We Hope You Rise Up

by

Students at Scriber Lake High School

We Hope You Rise Up

Cover Design: Jaycee Schrenk

Edited and compiled by Marjie Bowker, Ingrid Ricks and Dave Zwaschka

With Assistance from Danielle Anthony-Goodwin and Jennifer Haupt

Print book and eBook formatting by Hydra House

www.hydrahousebooks.com

Published by Scriber Lake High School
A program by
www.WriteToRight.org

This book is dedicated to our principal, Kathy Clift,
who has always believed in us and our stories.

TABLE OF CONTENTS

Some student authors worked with writing coaches to help them complete their stories.

OUR INTENTION WITH THIS STORY COLLECTION

W e have come together within this book. Although our stories are not the same, we all have something in common: we are striving. Life has thrown obstacles in our paths, but we have managed to grow from these experiences. We have accepted that we can't change the past and where we go from here is up to us.

We write hoping you understand, hoping you don't judge us—because we know you have a story, too. A story that should not have to define you. We write to bring hope, to show the ones who are too scared to come forth that they are not alone. We write to explain that even when life gets you down, it is important to keep your head high as well as your feet on the ground.

BROKEN PROMISES

SANTINO DEWYER

I can feel my face getting warm. My hands shake as I read the words.

Dear Jeronimo,

Remember my mom Yvonne, or me, your son? I really want to see you. Please come to my house or you could say my mom's house. Here's the address: _____ __th Avenue, _____, WA. I'm ten years old now.

Sincerely, Santino

I stand up and walk toward the kitchen. My mom is grabbing something out of the fridge. I'm still looking at the letter when I say, "Ma, look what I found." She turns around and pauses in front of me. I hand her the piece of paper.

"Yeah," she says. I can tell she doesn't know what else to say. She has a look of pity on her face. We both just stand there silently, looking at the piece of paper. I break the silence.

"Alright, well…" I sigh. My mom fixes her sparkling green eyes on me as I say, "Fuck that bitch."

I laugh, but my heart aches. My mom remains silent, just looking at me. I take the paper from her hand. I don't like awkward moments.

I head to my bedroom, shut the door behind me and take a seat on my black metal bunk bed. It creaks like it does when anyone touches it. Damn, it's annoying. I can't take my eyes off the letter. Every word hits like a punch to the face. I try to keep my hands from shaking but it's like they have a mind of their own. The day when I first met Jeronimo comes back to me, haunting me.

"Santino, Santino, honey wake up." My mom's voice was so kind I almost didn't mind her waking me up so early. I opened my eyes slowly and sat up, holding my body with my two arms. My mom was kneeling to the left side of the mattress, smiling. She was wearing a black sweater and blue jeans and had put on her usual purple lipstick and some mascara.

"What?" I asked.

She turned her head to look at someone who was in front of me. With the most gentle and motherly tone she replied, "This is your dad."

I followed her gaze. At the edge of the mattress was a Hispanic man. He was kneeling beside me, smiling. I could see my cousins and my Tia Wedda standing outside the bedroom. They were smiling, too.

I knew right then that this was my dad, my real dad. It was strange because I had always thought about what I would say to him when I finally met him. Now he was right in front of me, but I was so tired. And out of so many things that a ten-year-old could say to his father for the first time, all I could think to say was, "What's up?"

He made no reply. He just kept smiling. Everyone was quiet, staring at me, expecting me to say more. But I had nothing. What else could I say?

"Can you guys leave so he can get ready?" my mom finally said, breaking the silence. Jeronimo nodded his head, still smiling. He stood up and left, closing the door behind him. My mom reached into a plastic bag and pulled out a button-down shirt and a pair of blue jeans.

"Here, put these on," she told me, handing me the jeans. She knelt in front of me and I could smell her flowery scented perfume.

Next she handed me a button-down shirt. As I put my arms through the sleeves and she buttoned the buttons, I could feel my hands shake. It felt as if electricity was running through my veins. This wasn't a dream, no matter how unreal it felt. It was all happening so fast.

"We called him early this morning," my mom explained. "We told him not to come this early, but he wanted to see you so bad."

I didn't know what to say to that. I was still rubbing the eye boogers out of my eyelashes. When she finished buttoning my shirt, she grabbed a brush and some styling hair gel out of the bag. She opened the gel bottle and squirted some into her palm. I chuckled when it made a fart noise. She rubbed her hands together and ran her fingers through my hair. The gel felt cold and wet against my scalp, the slimy texture tickling the top of my forehead. Then she brushed the tip of my hair up as if it were a wave. When I looked in the mirror, I had to admit I looked good.

"Are you ready?" she asked. My hands were sweating. I took a long deep breath in, then out. I nodded. I was ready.

I followed her out of the bedroom and found him sitting on a bed in the next room. Everyone else must have decided to leave us alone. I could hear them upstairs in the living room watching movies. He jumped to his feet when he saw me.

"Hi Santino," he said.

"Hi," I replied.

"How are you?"

"Good." I was forcing myself to think of more things to say, better things, but I couldn't seem to think of anything. What could you say to someone you didn't even know?

My mom broke the awkward silence. "Santino, honey, is it okay if Jeronimo and I talk a little bit?"

She walked over to my bedroom and he followed. I walked over to join them, but my mom turned and faced towards me.

"No Santino, I mean alone," she said.

I stepped back as she closed the door behind her. I didn't really mind, just as long as they finished soon. I turned away from the door and sat on the same bed he had been sitting on.

I stared at the ceiling, stared at the floor. I walked around in circles and stared out the window. What was taking so long? Fifteen minutes went by. The sunshine emerged from over the rooftops and invaded the room with a golden glow. I stared at the bedroom door. What could they be talking about that could take this long?

Another fifteen minutes went by. I had finally met my father and our time together was being wasted by my mom and him talking. I wanted to ask him so many questions. He was still a stranger and I wanted to fix that.

Finally I heard a clicking noise. I turned quickly and found my mom and him exiting the bedroom. I jumped to my feet. My mom walked over beside me, and Jeronimo walked to the opposite side of the room. They didn't say a word. He finally broke the silence, "So, Santino, when should we hang out?"

I felt like I'd been slapped in the face. "Well, why not now?" I asked, trying to keep my voice from shaking.

My mom stepped forward. "Well, Santino, last night he was out with some friends. They were drinking. He's been up all night and he needs some sleep. You guys can hang out next weekend. I already gave him my number. He'll call next week, okay?"

It felt as if all the air had been knocked out of me. I stood staring at the ground. "Okay," I replied in a low shaky voice. But really it wasn't.

Today was the day I finally met my dad and my mom had decided to use all the time for herself. I didn't even get a chance to ask him any questions. My eyes started to sting, but I held the tears back. I wasn't going to cry in front of my dad. I had to man up.

"Yes, I'll call next week. I promise," he assured me. "It was very nice to meet you. See you next week."

I watched him turn and make his way up the stairs. I heard the front door open and close. I ran upstairs into the living room and jumped onto the couch, placing myself on my knees. I watched him get into his black pickup truck from the window behind the couch. I pushed the curtains aside to get a better view of my dad driving away.

I watched the car until it disappeared behind a pine tree. I jumped off the couch and ran back downstairs and sat back on the bed. I paid no attention to my surroundings. I fixed my eyes to the floor. My eyes stung as they filled with tears. I couldn't hold them in anymore. My heart felt as if it had been thrown out into the road and run over. As I blinked, my tears began to fall to the floor. Why did my mom have to steal my time with him?

That week I imagined all the things we would do together. I saw us at the fair going on rides that would make me puke, eating cotton candy, having a great time. But it was just a fantasy. I waited for a call that never came.

"Mama, has he called yet?" I asked my mom over and over.

"No. He's probably busy with work," she always replied. "Maybe he'll call next week." But even she sounded unsure. I waited for next week, and then the next week, and then the next week. There was no call. Then finally I realized there was never going to be a call. He had broken his promise. Those dreams I had were crushed. How could a person leave his son? Every time I thought about it my heart ached. Why didn't he want me?

✦

I'm still staring at the note I wrote to Jeronimo all those years ago. I don't want to put it back in that tote full of family pictures and albums. It doesn't belong there.

I grab my school backpack propped next to my bunk bed, pull the zipper, and open it. I reach inside and take out my white binder. It carries some pictures from when I'm younger so I can remember good times when I'm bored in class and because girls like to see my baby pictures.

I fold the letter back into a square and slip it into my binder behind a picture of my little brother, Carlos. Even though the letter brings back painful memories, it also reminds me of the boy I once was. The boy who was happier than he is now and who believed everything in this world was good. The boy who just wanted his father.

✦

A Note from Santino

I haven't seen Jeronimo since the day I met him. When I turned sixteen my mother found him on Facebook and discovered he was living in Vancouver, BC. When I contacted him we chatted on Facebook for a little while, but it didn't go so well. I now go to Scriber where I'm just trying to graduate. After that I plan to go to art school or a university to become an artist and an art teacher. I never was really good in school, but at Scriber I've become someone I never thought I'd be. In the future I'm gonna be the father that my father never was. My message to you: whether you are a parent or plan to be one, never leave your child. He needs you more than you think.

"If you live for people's acceptance, you will die from their rejection."—Lecrae

Artist: Santino Dewyer

GROWING APPETITE

JAYCEE SCHRENK

Marysville, WA

Eat! Get the hell off the couch and feed yourself! I think. But I continue to stare at the TV on the dusty coffee table.

I watch voluptuous, over-tanned girls with black bird's nest hair stumble and curse their way around the streets of Jersey and wish my fourteen-year-old self was there instead of here.

I'm sitting in the same spot where my mom left me three days ago when she went to do a drug deal—in a house owned by a stranger. I haven't slept, bathed or eaten. My hair feels slimy and my body odor creeps into my nostrils. The smell reminds me to light up another cigarette. My stomach gurgles and it feels as though it's eating the little body fat I have left.

Eventually my mom stumbles through the door in a grey sweat suit, her hair in a bun, looking almost as gruesome as I feel.

"There you are!" she says, slurring her words as she falls into the couch cushion beside me.

"What are you talking about?" I reply. As I turn to face her, I can tell she's already fallen into her high. Her eyes roll into the back of her head, closing slowly. She nods off, lifting her head up and down.

"Hello?! Is anyone there?" I scream as I push her body to the floor. She opens and shuts her eyes, cycling in and out of consciousness.

Tears fill my eyes as I jump off the couch. I grip my wrist with my nails and squeeze tight, trying to mask the pain of being forgotten by my own mother. I need to convince myself to calm down and know she still loves me. But anger overwhelms me and I kick the coffee table. The sting of my toes relieves the ache in my stomach.

I turn to my mom, wishing I could punch her out of her addiction. I settle for the wall above her head instead.

I sit down on the cold floor and open her purse to look for money. Her eyes open wide. She jumps up and rips her purse from my grasp.

"Stop going through my shit!" she screams, her eyes glossy and alert.

"Yeah, I'm pretty fucking hungry so you're going to give me the money that I know you have, or the EBT card," I say, my voice stern. I want her to understand how badly I'm hurting.

"Not my problem," she says in a sarcastic tone. "I don't have any money for you." She places the purse under her head to be used as a pillow. Within seconds she falls asleep again.

My mom has been a heroin addict for more than a year now. Ever since leaving my dad for abusing her, she's moved us seventeen times into strangers' apartments. I barely remember a kind face anymore; they all look the same.

"Feed me! Fucking feed me, I'm begging you! Please, Mom," I say as I pound my hands on the wood floor. The door creaks open and Tiffany, our latest "host," stumbles out of the dark hallway. I haven't seen her since I've been here. Tiffany's drug of choice is meth.

"What's going on, ladies?" she says nonchalantly as she grabs her bright green bra off the kitchen table. I wonder if she notices the tears dripping down my face or the clothes that hang on my back because I rarely eat. I wonder if she even cares.

'Please, Tiffany, I know I don't know you well but please, please buy me food," I plead. "I'll pay you back. I'll work it off. I'm good for my word. Ask anybody."

She rolls her green eyes and brushes her long brown hair back behind her ears as she takes a long drag of a menthol cigarette. She exhales and says, "No can do, hun. But I have something to take the ache away, if it's really that bad."

You are a drug dealer who doesn't have any spare money? Yeah, that sounds believable.

Her smile turns into a smirk as if she's challenging me. I nod in acceptance.

We walk through the kitchen into a pitch-black room. Her windows are covered with electrical tape and clothes are piled everywhere. A garbage bag full of empty soda cans, cigarette cartons and tin foil with dark lines and burn marks sits in the corner. She turns the lamp on, opens a drawer and pulls out a meth pipe with a tube taped around the jagged rim; it's stuffed inside a Coke can halfway-filled with water. It almost looks like a marijuana bubbler. She laughs to herself and peers at me with squinted eyes.

I return a nothing gaze.

"Sorry it's a little ghetto, but for your first time, lets add some flavor." She drops two cherry Jolly Ranchers into the soda can.

I had already done my share of drugs. I started drinking and smoking pot at twelve and had started a crazed ecstasy, molly, and coke binge over the summer. I had also taken prescription drugs from a bottle with a stranger's name on it. But I never thought I would do meth. I've had many opportunities to smoke before, but this time I'm not scared. I'm not worried about the outcome anymore.

"I'll light it for you so your hit isn't burnt to shit," she explains. "Just twist slowly."

She hands me the bubbler. I hesitate for just a moment. I wonder if I even care about myself at all anymore. My answer is obvious as I grab the thin glass, twist and inhale.

My body instantly feels warm and safe. I no longer resent Tiffany for refusing to spare me a few dollars. Suddenly, I feel love for her, for the air I breathe, for my mom. I feel content with every thought racing through my head.

"Exhale! It's not weed, don't hold it in!" Tiffany scolds. She grabs the bubbler out of my hand and places a small piece of meth into the clear glass bubble. I exhale my hit and a cloud dances across the room, making my gaze a fog. I gasp for fresh air, but settle for the lingering meth residue.

"Good shit, right?" Tiffany asks. I nod my head. Tiffany hits the pipe.

"Are you down to go on a run for me, girl?" she asks. I nod. "I got to get ready to go to the Indian reservation tonight to score some brown. Just go to Fred Meyers, he'll be waiting for you on the corner." She throws a small dope baggie on my lap, stands up and heads to the shower.

I know my legs are moving as I walk through the kitchen, but I can't feel them. I can hear my heart pounding in between the steps I take out the front door. The bright streetlight in the distance guides me as walk through the pitch-black darkness of the field. I sink into the mucky grass, my feet heavier with each step up the small hill that leads to the icy road. I stand under the streetlight and watch the fog of my breath evaporate into the dark of the night. I wait at the corner of the parking lot and stare across the street at the huge 7-11 sign beaming on top of the small convenience store. Footsteps approach behind me. I turn and greet a tall Native American man wearing a red hoodie and black sweatpants.

"Hey youngster, you Tiffany's girl?" he mumbles deeply. I nod and smile, too shy to reply with words. He pulls a 100-dollar bill from his pocket and we exchange money for the heroin.

"Catch you around," he yells as he runs to a truck parked nearby. He throws up a peace sign to signify our deal is done.

My walk back to Tiffany's feels long. I'm sweating and panting, even though it's winter and I'm only wearing an oversized t-shirt, sweatpants and short winter boots with no socks.

If I took off with this money, would my mom look for me? Would she even care?

When I get back my mom is still passed out. Food crosses my mind as I glance at the bill in my hand, but my aching appetite is gone.

Tiffany must have heard me come in because she yells,

"There's something on the coffee table for your troubles. Come bring me the money!"

I tiptoe past the dirty laundry piled up next to the bathroom and toss the money into her lap.

"Thanks," she mumbles as I walk back to the living room.

On the coffee table I find the bubbler and a dope baggie full of thick clear pieces of meth. I load the bubbler and learn to smoke on my own. The glass burns the tips of my fingers as I twist it back and forth, waving the flame under the glass. I bring it closer and further which makes my hit taste like burnt chemicals. I exhale the stale white smoke.

My appetite is gone but my stomach still growls. My legs are restless; they bounce viciously up and down. I start to count the bounces as my boredom grows more intense. I pace around the house and decide to scrub the moldy gunk stuck to the dishes and place them inside the dishwasher.

Finally my energetic boredom forces me to pull out a lined piece of paper, colored pencils, and an eraser. Staring at the paper, I can't think of anything but that the lines are not the same width apart. I sit in the same spot on the couch, coloring, smoking a substance that never appealed to me before today, feeling more content with my life than I have in years.

A Note from Jaycee

I dropped out of school in 8th grade due to my mother's addiction. My own addiction left me struggling, so I made what is now one of the biggest regrets of my life: to drop out my freshman year, too. I spent every day getting high with my mom and her friends. Some school friends stopped talking to me, while others used with me. By then I weighed 92 pounds and felt my life spiraling out of control. I couldn't look at myself in the mirror anymore; there wasn't much to look at. Soon my family started to notice my habits and turned from me as well.

I decided the first day of that summer—when I should have been entering my sophomore year—I would change my ways and get clean. I decided to be in my father's custody. I begged my mom to stop her addiction, but she only left me disappointed by using for another year. I felt obligated to shun her from my life. The summer I spent getting clean was filled with lonely days as I sat with my grandma on the patio with books and tea. Every day she encouraged me to get back to school and to get my head straight because I was soon to be sixteen and couldn't spend my days bumming around the house. I couldn't be more grateful for her influence in my life. That summer was three years ago; that summer is a summer I'll never forget.

Today I am eighteen. Tiffany is in prison, my mom has been clean for two years and I will graduate this spring, then head to college. I haven't decided my profession just yet but I am interested in becoming a midwife, a lawyer or a forensic psychiatrist.

"When I accept myself I am freed from the burden of needing you to accept me."—Steve Maraboli

THE EVIL WITHIN

KENNY G. KELLY

It feels as if my heart is going to jump out my throat and slap me silly, but I have a friend–who's like my brother–counting on me so I have to concentrate. I hear his voice slice through my thoughts like the tip of a blade.

"Hey Bro, there. He go right there," he says as he takes another hit from his cigarette.

I see the guy I'm about to ruin exiting the store and I start making my way toward him. I can see the fear in his girlfriend's face as she holds his hand and pulls him closer. I continue closing in on him and can see the fright build in his eyes as I pull my black bandana over my face.

"What's up?" I hiss as I swing my fist toward his head. He stumbles back a little, stunned. His girlfriend's screams almost blow out my eardrums. I feel my body heat up and the nervousness leaves. Then my anger takes over and I can't hear anymore. I'm like a bomb about to blow, like a killer who has just been let loose. I feel my fist crash into to his bony face, carrying with it all the rage that has built up inside me.

I was sitting with my two older brothers in the living room. It was dark out but our lights didn't work because my mom couldn't pay the electricity bill.

"When is she coming home?" my ten year-old brother asked. "It's been two hours since she left. I thought she was going to bring us food."

As soon I heard the word "food" I could feel the pain in my stomach. We hadn't eaten in two days because my mom didn't have money for groceries. My brothers and I had looked through all the cabinets in the kitchen, but there was nothing.

Another hour passed before my mom walked through the door. I could smell the cheeseburger as soon as she entered the living room. I rushed toward her and grabbed her leg.

"Mom, please can I have it? I'm so hungry. *Please*." I reached for the McDonald's bag but she yanked it out of my hand.

"Hold on," she said. "I only had enough money for one. We've got to share this equally because your brothers are hungry, too."

I wanted to scream that it wasn't fair to have to share a single cheeseburger. But I knew she was right.

I watched as she walked over to the dinner table, unwrapped the cheeseburger and pulled out a knife from a kitchen drawer. Even though I was only five years old, I could have eaten four of them.

She cut it into quarters.

"Go ahead. Take a piece," she said.

I ate it, then said, "I'm still hungry. Is there any more?"

"No son," she answered. "That's it. That's all we could afford."

A crowd has gathered around me to watch the fight. The guy's girlfriend is screaming for me to stop and out of the corner of my eye, I see my friend—the one who started all of this. He is rushing toward us. He grabs the guy from behind in a headlock, spins him and throws him to the ground. I look down at the guy, who appears ready to pass out. That's when I kick him hard in the ribs.

"Kids, pack your stuff. We can't live here anymore."

The stress in my mom's voice scared me.

"What happened?" I asked. "Why, Mama? I don't wanna go."

"Someone sold the house," she replied. "We've got to leave."

I went to the room I shared with my two brothers, grabbed my backpack, and shoved my shoes and clothes into it. My brothers followed. None of us spoke. I don't know what they were thinking, but I was too confused to think.

A half hour later, we were all sitting in our turquoise Pontiac, driving toward a shelter my mom had found in Tacoma.

She had told us a shelter was kind of like a hotel where people who didn't have anywhere else to live stayed. I spent the hour-and-a-half drive staring out the window. My mind was racing. *Would the people be nice at the shelter? Would there be kids my age? What would our room be like? Would it really be like a hotel? What if they didn't like us? Would we have to live on the streets?*

We arrived at the cement building at 10:34 p.m. I knew this because I saw a big clock on the wall as soon as we walked in. There was a small reception office in the lobby with a pretty blonde lady seated at the desk.

She looked us over.

"Are you the ones who called about the room?" she asked.

My mom nodded.

"Okay," she said, standing up from her desk. "Follow me."

We followed her down a long hallway with dirty white walls. We passed by lots of doors that I assumed led to other rooms. We arrived at a steep staircase and started climbing up the stair. As we climbed, the light got dimmer and dimmer. I had hoped this place would be like a Motel 6. But it wasn't like that at all. It felt uncomfortable and creepy. I just wanted to go home.

At the top of the first flight of stairs, I saw a window that looked out at a small playground. I could make out a slide and a few swings in the dark. We entered a hallway that circled the playground like a maze and took another flight of stairs. These stairs were even darker and creepier than the first set.

At the top of the stairs was a door to our room. The blonde woman inserted a key to unlock it. I still held out hope that our room would be like a Motel 6 with a TV, microwave, mini-fridge and a couple of queen beds. But it was nothing like that.

It was a tiny room. Against the left wall was a metal bunk bed that looked like it was ready to collapse. A small wooden dresser leaned against the right wall. That was it for furniture. The floor was dusty and stained with something sticky and dark, like someone had spilled Coke.

"There's no TV allowed in here," the woman said. "And both kids and adults have to be in the room with lights off by 10 p.m."

Her words made me angry. Why couldn't we have a TV? And why did we have to turn off the lights at 10 o'clock? This place was like a prison, not a motel.

As soon as she left, we climbed onto the bunk beds with our clothes still on. I went to sleep, too tired to think or care.

⚜

"Get off of him! Get off of him!" I see a tall, stocky guy coming at my friend. He kicks him in the leg, trying to get him to release his hold on the guy on the ground. Just then, a friend of my friend hits the tall, stocky guy in the face. Chaos erupts around me but the demon still has control. I look down at the guy on the ground and kick him in the face.

⚜

"You're a faggot. You are not my son!" my dad screamed as he drove me toward the house where my mom was staying. "I can't have a son that is such a faggot. If you want your mom, fuck you. You can have her."

A half-hour before, my dad had arrived out of the blue at the house where I was staying with my mom. I was still asleep when he came into the room. "Come on. Get up. We've got to go," he said.

I was confused. I didn't even know he knew I was staying there. My mom and I had been spending nights at different friends' homes because we had nowhere else to go.

I threw on my clothes and followed him to the car. I couldn't even say goodbye to my mom because she was at a doctor's appointment.

"Where are we going?" I asked as I got into his burgundy-purple Saab.

"We're going home," he replied. I'd lived with my dad on and off for the past couple of years because CPS had gotten involved and decided I was better off with him. But I missed my mom and loved her to death, so I spent weekends with her and had decided to stay with her despite the court orders.

I felt the familiar anger and pain. My dad scared me, so usually I kept quiet. But I was nearly fourteen and decided it was time to stand up for myself.

"No. I want to go back to my mom," I replied firmly. "I don't want to leave her. I want to go back."

My dad hit the brakes, made a U-turn and started heading back toward the house. That's when he started screaming at me. He'd never spoken to me that way before and his words were like knives jamming into my gut. The tears rolled down my face, which only increased my dad's rants.

"You can fucking have her," he spit at me. "Don't ever talk to me or call me again. I'm not your dad anymore. And you will never be a son of mine." He pulled up to the house he'd picked me up from a few minutes before. "Get the fuck out of my car!" he said.

I was so hurt it was hard to breathe. I opened the passenger door, ran up the steps through the door, and down the hall to the safety of our friend's bedroom.

❖

Sirens snap me out my rage.

"The cops are coming, Bro," my friend yells. "Come on. Let's go."

He starts running and I'm right behind him. We race to an apartment complex and hide in the basement stairwell.

We can still hear the sirens, but they sound more distant. *What did I just do? Why did I beat him up like that? He didn't do anything to me. I didn't even know him. What about me? What's going to happen to me? What will my mom think?*

I think about school. The fight has taken place over lunch and there are still two periods left to go. I have to get back so I won't miss class—and so people won't suspect me.

I take off my black coat and gold-and-black Mac Dre shirt, leaving only my white T-shirt.

"Hey, Bro. I'm going back to school," I tell him.

"Alright, Bro. Just be safe," he replies.

I'm shaking a little as I walk the half-mile back to school. *What is happening to me? Who am I?*

I don't know the answer. But I realize as I re-enter the school that I am not the same Kenny everyone thought they knew.

❖

A Note from Kenny

The rage that took over me that day taught me a valuable lesson: that I carried a lot of anger inside of me and I needed to dig deep and face it so it could never control me again. Now when the rage hits, I've learned to walk away, count, even meditate. It makes all the difference. Though my family has been poor all of my life, I now look at it as a gift. We had nothing but each other and it has created a bond that can never be broken. I've learned that when you have a family who loves you, you have everything. I'm now a nineteen year-old senior at Scriber. When I graduate, I want to join the music industry with my older brother, Robert, and become a famous rapper. I have lots of dreams and know I'm going down in the history books. Everything I am I owe to my mom. She's done so much for me and has always told me that whatever I dream, I can do.

"Hope is being able to see that there is light despite all of the darkness." — *Desmond Tutu*

HUNTING FOR A REASON

DESTINY ALLISON

"One more time," the nurse says. "You're almost done."

I squeeze my boyfriend's hand as hard as The Hulk for that one last push. I've anticipated this day for months, but he's finally almost here. I finally get to meet him. A feeling of relief spreads through my whole body and the next thing I know my son is on my chest. In the background I hear my mom's soft, calm voice. Her words flow together in the most perfect manner.

"He is so precious, honey. You did an amazing job, Destiny."

Her words are followed by another comforting voice, my grandma's.

"Sweetie, he is so cute. I am so proud of you."

The more they talk, the more blurred their sweet, heart-warming voices get. I am trembling, hoping nobody notices my nerves. I can't hear a word they say because I am too in love to apply my attention to anything other than my angel. I feel strange, abnormal, but I know what I'm feeling is love. It's an unconditional love I never knew existed, and with each moment I hold my son the feeling gets stronger, creating an even more unbreakable bond. I can feel it growing bigger within my chest. It is a love that can do no wrong.

Looking into my arms, that feeling of exquisiteness begins to fade. The pit of my stomach begins to cramp from the guilt I feel for my previous doubts about whether or not to keep him.

I sat next to my mom in the Everett Planned Parenthood, getting whiffs of the permanent coffee smell that lingered around her. As I watched her fiddle with her phone, it took all my focus to keep breathing. The waiting room smelled of cleaning supplies, latex, and hand sanitizer, the same way my normal doctor's office smelled. There were girls to my left and right dressed in sweats and baggy jackets, just like me. Some had boyfriends with them but most were alone. I began to shake and my breathing became heavier.

"Destiny Allison." I looked up to see a nurse holding the door open with her body.

"Destiny Allison," she repeated. I got up and slowly walked towards her. The eyes of everyone in the waiting room were on me, but I kept my eyes on the nurse and stared at her curly, chestnut-brown hair, trying to forget that all these people knew what I was about to do.

"Take your shoes off and step on here," she said. I followed her instructions and stepped onto the scale. "How are you?" she asked. The scale read 98.3 pounds. "Wow you're really small."

"Yeah, I get that a lot," I said with a slight stutter.

Her voice was calm, like she wasn't nervous at all, as if she had done this a million times before. Maybe because she had. She walked me into my room. The walls were mostly bare, but the few posters hanging on the wall were where I focused my attention. I didn't want to listen to her because I didn't want to know anything about how the abortion worked. I wanted to get it over with and forget it ever happened.

"Have you thought about your decision? You know the other options and have talked to somebody else about it?" Her voice had a hint of concern as she questioned me.

How could this happen to me? This only happens in movies. We were careful. I'm only sixteen. I can't be a mom yet, I can barely take care of myself—let alone another human being. I have to do this. I can't back out now. I'm not ready to be responsible for another life. This is what I'm obligated to do.

"Yes, I'm sure," I said with a quiet voice, hoping she wouldn't hear the anxiety through my three words.

"Okay, we just have to ask so you know you have other options; however, because you're sure we will keep going. Once I leave the room, I need you to undress from the waist down. There's a blanket you can cover yourself with right there. I will be back in a couple minutes."

She closed the curtain and left the room.

I was alone with my nerves; I wished my mom could be in the room with me. *Why wouldn't they let her come back here?* I tripped over myself trying to take my shoes off. I collected myself and slipped the rest of my clothes off and sat on the table with the blanket over me.

My mind raced as I waited for the nurse to come back. *I can do this. Just don't think about it. It will be over soon and you* won't *ever have to deal with it again.* My thoughts were interrupted by a knock on the door. The nurse was back. It was time.

I lay on the table with the lower half of my body covered by the blanket.

"Before we do the procedure, I have to do a vaginal ultrasound to see how far along you are. It's going to be a bit uncomfortable, but it will be over fast."

"Okay," I whispered. My whole body shook at this point. I just wanted my mom.

"Do you want to see the baby?" she asked as she stared up at the screen.

Destiny, you can't look. If you look you might love. If you love you might change your mind. You have to do this. I shook my head "no" even though my heart was screaming at me to say "yes."

"All right, that's all. I just have to run these next door so someone else can take a look at them."

She was gone. I was all alone again. I fiddled my thumbs and swung my feet back and forth to pass the time until she returned.

When she knocked again my heart didn't race and my breathing didn't get heavier—it slowed. I was frozen. Something was wrong and I could sense it.

She finally spoke. "At our clinic we only do abortions up to thirteen weeks, and based on your ultrasound, we place you at fourteen and a half weeks."

In that moment the fear disabled me so badly that my heart skipped a beat and I missed a breath or two. My palms were sweaty, but the thing that gave away my panic was that I couldn't seem to keep my voice steady. *How was I too far along? There's no way that was possible. I'd been taking birth control for three months. That's why everybody said I hadn't been on my period. My body was just adjusting.*

My thoughts were shut off by my nurse's voice. "You still have options. We have some clinics that will do a procedure called a D and E abortion up to twenty weeks. These procedures take two days and you may have to stay at the hospital the first night. Would you like me to give you the information for those clinics?

No sound came out of my open mouth, so I just nodded my head and reached out my hand since she already had the paper ready for me. As if she knew I was going to say yes. She opened the heavy white door and I followed her back through the hall.

The hall seemed longer than the first time I walked through it. The pictures looked blurry, the scale by the door seemed taller, and the air felt heavier. It was as if the walls were closing in on me and planned on squishing me if I didn't walk fast enough.

She opened the door and there was my mom. She was sitting in a chair flipping through pages of a magazine. I could tell she was surprised to see me so soon. Her eyes looked just as confused as her voice sounded.

"What's going on?" she asked.

How am I going to tell her when I can't even believe it myself?

"Let's go, Mom. I'll explain in the car."

The nurse grabs her Expo marker and asks his name. "Hunter Luke Knudsvig," I say proudly as I observe the biggest blessing I could have received. His hair is blonde and short like peach fuzz, his skin softer than a feather. His eyes are cement grey with a ring of crystal blue on the outer lining. He is perfection.

My boyfriend's hand runs down my arm and I am forced to wash the memory out of my mind.

"Destiny, are you okay?" he asks. I nod my head "yes," not wanting to tell him how woozy I feel from all the drugs, how I'm being haunted by the past. My baby is scratching my chest with his sharp, brittle nails. I can't help but smile down at him.

I was fifteen weeks pregnant, lying on my twin bed with my boyfriend of five months. My cheeks felt hot and my eyes puffy from all the tears that had streamed out of them and slid down my face.

"Adam, I can't do it. I can't take two days to kill my baby. It's a whole baby now with a full body."

His hazel eyes looked into mine. "Good. Because I was going to tell you I don't want you to do that. I watched some videos on how they do it and it's really bad."

He paused for a moment then continued.

"So what do we do now?"

"I can't carry a baby in my tummy for nine months, have the baby, and then just give my baby to someone else. I can't live my life knowing I have a child in this world being raised by someone else and I'm not involved at all." My hands became clammy and I could feel tiny drops of sweat start gather on my forehead. I was nervous about how he would react.

For a moment we sat in silence. He took a deep breath.

"Okay, Destiny, we're going to have a baby. We're going to be parents. I will get a job and support the three of us, and you can go to school. We will figure it out. We can do this. I love you."

I put my hand on my stomach, trying to hold back my smile as I said, "I love you, too." My heart felt content going forward with the life I was about to begin. I tried my hardest not to jump up and down with excitement. For the first time in so long, I felt genuinely happy.

The pain meds have made me loopy and tired. My body is lifeless, as if I've just run a marathon. My eyes are heavy, as if I haven't slept in days. My mouth is dry, as if I haven't had a drop of water in weeks. It takes all my effort to stay awake and socialize with the people who've come to visit me. Hunter is lying on my chest, sleeping, making a faint sucking noise. A tear falls off my face because I know that having my baby was the right choice. My reason to do good is finally in my arms.

But despite the euphoria I feel, there is also a sense of doubt. My mind tries to race out of my head. I'm only seventeen, with no job, and a relationship that is hanging by a string. I haven't graduated from high school and have no plan for my life. *What if I fail him? What if I am not capable of being the mother that he needs? What if I destroy him? Can I do this on my own? If Adam and I don't work out can I raise my son by myself?*

A small cry erases my negatives thoughts; I look down at Hunter and whisper, "Hunter, I am determined to give you the life you deserve, whatever it takes. I will always be here. You and I will be fine. I promise. I love you, Bug."

A Note from Destiny

Hunter is now a little over one and every day I get to spend with him is magical. He is the sweetest boy, and to this day I can't believe I almost gave up having him. Having a baby so young has been one of the hardest struggles in my life, but I wouldn't trade being his mother for anything in this world. His father and I realized that we weren't going to work out, but he continues to support both Hunter and me like he said he would. I have graduated from high school and I am taking some time to focus on Hunter, then plan to get a full-time job and look into colleges. My goal is to go to culinary school and one day own my own restaurant. I hope my story shows that no matter how hard or scary a situation may be, you can do anything if you want it badly enough and are willing to do what it takes to make it happen.

"In the flush of love's light we dare be brave / And suddenly we see that love costs all we are and will ever be / Yet it is only love which sets us free."—Maya Angelou

NO SUCH THING AS "GOODBYE"

BRIEAUNNA DACRUZ

I feel the warmth of my seven-year-old cousin, Emma, as I cradle her body against mine. I glance at the clock and my gut tightens. *How could this month be over already? How could it have gone so fast?* Emma shifts in my arms and I pull her closer. I don't want to let go, I don't want to say goodbye. But at least I know she's going to be okay.

As I pull her tighter my thoughts shift back to the day my world changed.

"Bri, come here."

By the low tone of my mom's voice, I knew something was wrong. When I saw the tears on her cheek, panic crept up inside me.

"Mom. What's wrong? What's going on?"

I took a seat beside her on the couch. She let out a sigh before speaking.

"Emma went to the doctor for her headaches today," she finally blurted. "Your cousin has craniopharyngioma."

Her words slammed into me. Fear and confusion took over and a million thoughts ran through my mind. *What is craniopharyngioma? What's wrong with Emma? Is she going to be okay?"*

My mom explained that craniopharyngioma is a tumor that develops near the pituitary gland. I was still confused. I didn't even know what a pituitary gland was. But the word "tumor" struck me instantly. I opened

Safari on my phone and typed in *craniopharyngioma*. My stomach felt like a bottomless pit as I read about her condition.

"Craniopharyngioma is a type of central nervous system tumor. A tumor can be cancerous or benign. A cancerous tumor is malignant, meaning it is usually fast-growing and can spread to other parts of the body."

It took getting to the end of those words before I felt the stress-sweat. *This couldn't be happening. Why her? She's just a kid.* They say never to think of the bad and always stay positive, but the negative thoughts cluttered my mind. I wanted to ask so many questions, but I knew no one could answer them.

"Everything will be okay, Bri. Please calm down."

I heard my mom's words but didn't acknowledge them.

Emma shifts in my arms again and I look into the face that is the spitting image of mine. I think about the day she was born, and the instant bond between us. The words from my family run through my mind: "She looks just like you, Bri. If we had a picture from when you were little you'd be amazed!"

"*I like to move it move it*" played on the TV screen hanging down from the middle of the car. We were on our way home from Raging Waters, an arrival gift my uncle had surprised me with after landing in Sacramento—the place I would call home for the next three weeks. As I listened to the music, I replayed my uncle's phone call from the month before in my mind.

"Bri, Emma needs surgery to remove the tumors," he began, his voice sounding tired and strained. "If we pay for a plane ticket, will you spend a few weeks helping babysit your cousins?"

I felt like I'd just won the lottery. *An expense-paid trip to California in the summer? Of course I wanted to go.* At the time, I wasn't thinking about what the trip really meant. To me, hanging out in California with my cousins sounded like a vacation.

"Of course. When would I be leaving?" I had replied in a cheerful tone.

The sounds of the song continued to blast through the car. To my left was my eight-year-old cousin, Isabella, and to my right was Emma. My body swayed to the music as I heard precious laughs come from both of them as they moved to the beat of Madagascar's catchy rhythm. I felt myself smiling. Everything seemed okay in this moment. Spending the day at the waterpark had been a fun start to the summer, but I knew that soon the fun would be over. I glanced at Emma, who was still laughing and moving to the music. If you didn't know she was sick, you'd never get the slightest hint. *Did she even know?*

Two days later I trailed behind my uncle, trying to fight the waves of worry that washed over me as I stepped into the elevator at Sutter Memorial Hospital. A doctor stood beside me, smiling, with a four-wheeled IV holder beside her. The veins in my arm began to pulse.

My uncle assured me that Emma's operation had gone fine, but I still didn't know what I was walking into. We entered the hallway of Emma's wing and I saw my uncle's friend exiting her room. My anxiety increased with each step.

Just breathe, Bri. Breathe.

The smell of disinfectant hit me the minute I stepped into her room. I saw monitors everywhere before my eyes locked on Emma. Her eyes were swollen shut and I could tell she wasn't conscious. A huge white bandage wrapped around the top of her little head. A green feeding tube came out of her left nostril and IVs covered her arm. Her slightly open mouth revealed her not-yet adult teeth. She looked as if she had been brutally beaten. Purple was her new skin color.

If this is what they consider "okay" to be, I wonder what they consider "bad?" My aunt sat beside her, holding her hand. I stared for a few more moments. *These people are blind,* I thought to myself as I walked to the far right side of her bed, leaned down, and gave her a kiss.

"I love you Emma," I whispered, though I knew she couldn't hear me. My heart pulsed out of my chest. "I'm going to the waiting room," I blurted. My uncle followed as I exited the room. My sight blurred and my knees weakened as I walked past a nurse toward the hallway. My vision went completely black and I felt my palms slam against the cold hospital floor.

My uncle's arm wrapped around me. "Do you need help? Are you okay? We're calling for help now."

He peppered me with questions. Soon I was surrounded by doctors who bombarded me with more pointless questions. I just wanted everyone to leave me alone. *Why were they bothering with me? Why didn't they take care of Emma?'*

"No," I answered firmly. "I don't need help. I'm going to be fine."

Seven agonizing days later, Emma was still in the hospital in the same room they placed her in after surgery.

"Hi Brieaunna," she said, smiling. It was the first time I had spoken to her since she had woken up. Her eyes were no longer swollen shut and the IVs and feeding tubes were gone from her arm and nostrils. The white bandage had been removed, too, so I could see where they had removed the tumor. Her incision, covered with stitches, was a few inches long.

My aunt tapped my shoulder. "Will you grab the iPad beside Emma, please?"

I handed it to her and she pulled up an app featuring animated fireworks. She placed the iPad on top of Emma's lap and we all surrounded her bedside to enjoy the fireworks together as a family. It was the 4th of July.

"Emma, do you like this?" I asked her.

"Yeah."

I could tell by her response she was drained. Ten minutes passed.

"My head hurts, turn it off," she pleaded.

By 6:30 that evening, she was ready for bed. We gathered up my cousins and piled in the car to head home. I kept to myself during the drive—texting, listening to music, whatever it took to make sure I was distracted from the sky.

If Emma wouldn't be seeing a fireworks display this year, neither would I.

⚜

"Bri, it's time to get going," my aunt says, interrupting my thoughts. "Your plane might leave without you if we don't get there soon."

I miss my family and friends back home and I am more than excited to see them. But now that it's time to go, I'm not ready to leave.

I look down at Emma, still snuggled in my arms. I know from the expression on her face that she doesn't want me to go, either.

"I have to catch my flight now, Emma," I say softly. "I promise I will see you soon."

When the words come out, I'm angry with myself. I live two states away, a whole eight hundred miles, and I've just promised a seven year-old girl I will see her soon because I'm too afraid to say goodbye.

I hope my "soon" isn't something she holds me to, because I've learned that days turn into weeks, weeks turn into months, and months eventually turn into years. I don't want to disappoint her. At the same time, saying goodbye sounds like forever and I know this is not a forever thing. I gaze into Emma's face and give her one final squeeze.

"I love you, Emma."

A Note from Brieaunna

As I read through this story that took place nearly two year ago, I still believe there is no such thing as "goodbye." Emma is now eight years old and will be turning nine on May 13. Since her surgery, she has gone through countless radiation treatments to continue reducing the size of the tumor. She has lost much use on her left side—mainly the function in her left arm. We thought the radiation and chemotherapy would help, but recently she had an MRI and the doctors say that her tumor has doubled in size. Our family is now waiting on the Gamma Knife doctor to let us know if Emma needs another surgery. The tumor is not affecting her at this moment and she continues to be just like any other eight-year-old child. Through this short story about the struggle we went through as a family and continue to go through each day, I hope you will gain strength and know that there is always hope. There is absolutely no such thing as "goodbye" unless that's what you choose.

"Life may not be the party we hoped for, but while we're here we should dance."—Unknown

Brieaunna Dacry

PARTY

JEFF KAUK

"Hey, little homie. You wanna do some shit with me and my cousin?" my friend asks.

It's close to 11 pm on a Friday night. I'm at a party in Lake Stevens at the grange—a small, old, rundown building. The party was put together by teenagers, but random adults always end up there, too. They come every week, and sometimes bring more friends. They aren't our parents, but look old enough to be. They get messed up like the rest of us. Every weekend a live punk rock band leads all of the pushing, shoving people with loud scream music in the mosh pit.

I'm here with my sister. She's 15—two years older than me—and she's dressed in a black, short skirt. We get along so well we're more like friends than siblings. She's standing next to her group of friends, and I'm next to mine. We're all smoking weed and having a great time.

My sister walks over to my group smelling of cigarettes, weed and perfume.

"Hey, kid, do you want to go smoke some spice with me and my friend?" she asks one of my friends.

He leaves to join them. That's when I run into my homie from school. He's a blonde kid who looks like he hates everyone because of the permanent scowl on his face. He has some cocaine, alcohol and weed with him. He pulls out his rolling paper, sprinkles some cocaine over the weed, rolls it up and passes it to me. I spark my joint while he rolls a few more so we don't have to struggle trying to roll one when we're high.

"Damn this is some good weed!" I say. He laughs.

"Why are you laughing?" I ask.

He looks at me blankly as if I don't know. Actually, I don't.

"There is some PCP sprinkled on that, bitch!" he says. At this point I've been using for six months. I've been smoking weed, drinking, popping pills, and dropping acid. But I've never tried PCP. I look at my joint and realize that it's just a stinger now so I can't turn back. We take a few sips from a bottle of whiskey.

My body begins to shake as strength from the adrenaline builds. I'm scared; I feel out of control and don't know what's going to happen next. After a few minutes of feeling intense fear, I'm able to relax and enjoy my high. I go outside and start messing with people.

After about forty minutes of the high, I begin to crash. I feel like I'm moving really fast but I know I'm not. My heartbeat slows down and I can barely walk. My brain's numb and everything is quiet in my head. My throat's numb. I see my sister walking back so I shuffle over to her and put my head on her shoulder. I never do this.

"What the fuck happened?" she yells. "Who did this to you? What are you on?"

She keeps asking me stuff but I can barely talk. She's trying to hold me upright. She doesn't know that I've been doing harder drugs for a few months—she thinks I've just been smoking weed and drinking. But weed doesn't numb me anymore and I need to be numb so I don't have to feel any pain.

Half the pain comes from my parents. My mom was absent and left us with my dad, who makes us feel like shit all the time and doesn't care. He's an angry person who takes his anger out on his kids. He always throws stuff at us—like the TV remote. He also throws us into walls. There's a time I always remember and it never goes away: I was at home and my dad and mom were arguing like always, but this time my dad got mad at me and my sister just because we happened to be standing in the hallway. He pushed us out of his way and we hit the ground.

The other half of my pain comes down to loss. When I'm not using drugs or drinking, all that pain sits in my mind and I don't know how to handle it.

I lean against the building as my sister stands next to me, watching to see if I'm going to come out of it. I close my eyes and hear voices, but I can't make out what they're saying. People huddle around and video me with their phones. Some of them laugh, but most are concerned and ask me what I need.

Someone says, "Call an ambulance." I hear someone else talking on the phone; eventually, I hear sirens.

My breathing is intense and my eyes are wandering everywhere in panic, but I can't move. I know I need to get out of there before the ambulance and the police arrive. I don't want to be anywhere near the police.

My sister tries to move me. "Come on, J, we got to go," she says in a shaky voice.

Her friend helps her get me up and they carry me to a school a few blocks away so we don't get in trouble. I feel heavy but I know they have me. They sit me down on the ground. I feel my heart stop and everything goes black. Suddenly I see my grandpa, who died earlier in the year—he's about twenty feet away, just looking at me. I know it isn't heaven because I can feel them moving me.

I wake up gasping for air. I open my eyes and we're moving again.

"Where are we going?" I ask.

My sister says something but I can't understand her. I'm thinking *Fuck, Mom's going to kill me*. We never get in trouble for this type of shit;

we usually get suspended from school for something stupid, like fighting or saying inappropriate things to teachers.

When we get back to the party the ambulance is gone. They sit me back down and someone asks if I want a drink or some food. I nod my head. I hear people yelling about finding food and water. My sister's friend gives me some chips and water. When a girl tries to take my chips, I open my eyes wide, yell "Fuck you!" and hit her.

"J, we have to go home soon so try to act normal because Mom is coming to get us," my sister says.

I start to hyperventilate. I just want to leave so I don't get in trouble. I get up after a few minutes, but it's hard. My legs aren't working. I see my mom pull up. I stay quiet in the car because I don't want her to know I'm high. I try so hard to stay awake.

When we get home, I go to my room and wait for my mom to go to bed. Suddenly I'm no longer tired. As soon as it's clear, I climb out of my first floor window so I can smoke a cigarette and fall to the ground. I pick myself up but can barely stand, so I lean against the house for support.

Nausea hits me out of nowhere and I puke. I grab the whiskey from my inside pocket and drink it to try to kill the emotions. I climb back through the window and finally crash.

I wake up late the next afternoon. My sister shows me a video of the night. I see myself deathly pale, slurring my words and nodding out. Then I see myself hit the girl over the chips and just laugh.

"Man that was a crazy night," I say to my sister.

She just scowls.

I don't tell anyone, including her, that my heart had stopped. That I had died and come back.

I don't tell anyone that I had seen my dead grandpa shaking his head in disappointment. He was the only one I could talk to—he always knew the right thing to say at the right time. He was my role model and I wanted to be as successful as he was in life.

I smell like weed, alcohol, cigarettes and puke. I hate myself for letting shit get out of hand. I just want to go lie in bed and tell everyone to fuck off.

I head to my friend's house to smoke a blunt. I am chuckling as I show her the video, even though it isn't funny.

"Jeff, you're stupid," she tells me.

"I know, believe me, I know."

A Note from Jeff

Since this happened I have changed my life completely. I'm clean and sober now and my parents have both changed for the better—my dad is a good father now. I'm planning to graduate on time after years of not taking school seriously. I have accomplished my goal of becoming a better person and student. I don't cause trouble, and now I do my work because I've realized that my life won't go anywhere acting like that. My goal is to join the Marines after I graduate. I want everyone to know that drugs and alcohol are never the answer to anything.

"Keep your head up."—Tupac

BLURS AND BEANS AND SHORT-LIVED THINGS

EMMA HESS

The bathroom of Alison's apartment is freezing. My stomach cowers underneath goose bumps as I set down the stick holding my ever-elusive future.

Two minutes. I watch it lying there with its smug pretentiousness as I wash my hands, slowly closing the door behind me.

Alison, my 23-year-old sister, ushers me to the couch as if I am a fragile box of memories that might unleash everything terrible if I stand up for too long. I don't blame her. The very fact that I've come to Alison after years upon years of absolute loathing is laughable. And look where I am. Sitting in the apartment she shares with her fiancé. Watching a Disney movie. Waiting to see a positive or a negative.

She must be reassuring me, but I can't hear her over the steady stream of the what-if's that pound into the meat of my brain. God, is she actually showing me a list of names she's thinking of for her future children? Timing, Alison, was never your forte.

What am I doing? I should be kissing her feet for being accommodating when I needed it most. What was it that I used to say? A painful past makes an unpleasant present? But anyways, who cares? It's not as if she can read my mind.

I look over at her warily.

She smiles. Prize-winning, even, and checks her phone. "One more minute."

Owen would have a fit if I'm pregnant. Not out of anger or regret, but out of shock. He's the kind of guy you hear about in movies and such: "the one who stays," "the one who cares," and of course, "the one who loves too much and seems kind of pathetic at first but dammit this man's a keeper."

My mom would cry, I think. Her being Mormon combined with a soft heart makes it easy to set off the waterworks.

And my dad? Shit. All I have to say is I don't want to be there when he finds out. *If.* I mean if he finds out. If there even *is* anything to find out. You know what I mean.

Alison looks at me when the timer goes off, her hair weaving around her eyelashes.

"Do you want me to check it?"

Of course I do.

She walks away while I glare at the light reflecting off of a glass of water on the coffee table. When did she put it there? Perhaps when my urine was streaming onto the plastic strip. Too much information?

It seems that the room is quiet. I feel suffocated by the second of silence between my breaths. But that can't be the case. "Let it Go" has been turned up to the point where the insides of my ears ache. My mind must've trapped me again. It does that.

She comes out. She's smiling. But the thing with the Hess family is that we laugh when it is completely inappropriate to do so. Our defense mechanism, if you will. So I've learned not to trust smiles.

I'm right not to.

"I don't know how to say it," she begins, "I mean, you're my little sister."

Blood means nothing if there is a lack of mutual respect. I almost tell her that. Except I am choked by disbelief. My head spins.

"Are you sure?" I ask. She hands it over. And there it is—the bright pink plus that seals my fate.

⁂

Owen doesn't react the way I expect him to.

We're sitting on his twin-sized bed with our hands clasped. The dark blue walls close in on me when I say the words.

At first he's quiet, his face vacant of any emotion. I nudge him a little, trying to prod out his thoughts.

"I knew it," he mumbles.

"What do you think about it?"

"What kind of question is that?" he cracks a grin and rubs his face with his hands. "It's just a lot to take in, I guess."

"You guess?"

"Emma," he flops backwards, pressing into the comforter with an exasperated sigh. "What are we going to do? What do you want to do?"

"I don't know. I mean, we have three things to choose from, really. Abortion, adoption or we can keep it."

Being around him makes me feel less tense. We met in September, and now—on Easter Sunday—we are faced with this. We've talked about the future often, as couples do, but neither of us saw this coming. Who would?

"What do you think of abortion?" His eyes hover over the blankets. The pang in my stomach reverberates.

"I can't do that. For one, I'd be overridden with guilt. Two, that'd make me more depressed than I already am. And three, my mom doesn't believe in that. I don't want her to hate me or something."

"Okay, so, you want to go into labor then?" It comes out as a sigh. Did I? Horror stories of pregnancies gone awry flip through my brain. I can almost feel my exhaustion from the baby's cries waking me up for the tenth time that night. Or maybe I'm just tired of thinking.

"Well, I don't know! I only just got the results!"

"It's okay, calm down." He takes my wrist and pulls me down next to him, wrapping his arm around my shoulders. I sigh as he speaks. "We'll take it one step at a time, okay?"

"Okay," I lay my head on his shoulder. "When should I tell my parents? Wait, when are you going to tell yours?"

"I'll probably tell my mom first, because I'm closer to her and then meet up with the rest of my family individually." It is a well-known fact that he and his father are distant; I guess I didn't know how much until now.

We shrug back into the bed, our legs intertwined, his hand on my stomach. His disbelief has changed into a patient acceptance. We are watching—but not really, as you can imagine—a movie. Whatever it is, something one of the characters says makes an impression on him. I only know this because he looks at me with sober, honest eyes and whispers, "Let's keep it. We can do this."

Later that night, I explain the situation to my mom.

"Have you told anyone else?" she asks, her voice shaking.

"Only you, Ali and Owen know."

"Tell your father soon. I don't want him to find out from the wrong sources."

There is something about her request that makes it hard for me to nod. Dad and I used to be really close. Memories of scooter rides and Richmond Beach pop into my head. We used to watch football games together. I was always the first person he'd ask when he needed someone to accompany him anywhere. But over the years, our relationship had withered away and was replaced by arguments, uncomfortable silences, and lectures about how I needed to live my life. He was beginning to get more stressed from work, often leading him to shout about personal problems to the rest of the family. What if he did that when I told him?

Husbandland (the incredibly idiotic name someone came up with for the bottom floor of our house) is a mess as always. The dogs has ripped up another Santa hat and the red remains are scattered across the floor like intestines, which compliments the puke green leather couches layered with piss-smelling blankets. I guess the name does fit.

Mom, my sisters Alison, Elle and I (don't ask me how Elle knows, I didn't tell her—I suspect mom) sit on the thrones of discomfort, waiting for Dad to come out of the bathroom.

Earlier that day I'd gone to Denney Court for the third—fourth?—time. The Becca Law has been woven ever-so-gently into my life. If you don't know what it is, you're lucky. Basically they lecture you about not going to school enough, making you feel like an absolute twat by the end of it. I cried on my first visit, and by the second I was about ready to rip the hair off of the judge's head.

The funny thing is, the judges always asked me why I missed school, and whatever I told them they'd say "Excuses!" Yes, sir. That's what you asked for. The reason? Depression, bone-rattling social anxiety, the bullying, vultures dressed as teachers, the constant hum of collective disappointment whenever I visited the counselor to check my "progress," stress, not wanting to come in late and have to see that godforsaken attendance office, sitting at lunch accompanied only by books, presentations I'd finished but couldn't for the life of me give in front of the class so I avoided the teachers, seeing that person everyday who made my life hell and took pride in it, feeling so fucking alone all the fucking time and feeling like complete and utter shit about everything I've ever done. Like I could never amount to anything because I was too stupid.

And, after I told my therapist that I wanted to keep it, she said that it might be good for my mental health. That maybe it was a blessing in disguise. Maybe I could focus my energy so much on the baby that I wouldn't have anything else on my mind. It'd give me a reason to keep going. It'd make me stronger. I'd break out of my shell by speaking with doctors, facing my fears of criticism head-on by strangers' vivid opinions of me. My joy replaced depression as I saw its tiny perfect face light up with a grin.

Maybe I can get through this. Maybe I will really be okay.

And I keep thinking that until Dad walks out of the bathroom and into the room, wiping his hands on his pant legs.

Mom stirs, laughing a little in spite of herself. She taps her fingers in anticipation, sending ripples of wings into my stomach. "So, we went to court today." Perhaps not the best way to start.

Dad groans. "What'd she do now?"

"It was very informal." And thus begins them talking about me as if I'm not there. I don't really listen, trying hard to ignore the glow of anger steaming atop his head. There is an instantaneous moment where I feel my face start to boil under the pressure of his emotions.

With a pause between her words, I hear her say, "There's something else."

"What now?" he hisses. "Is she *pregnant too?*"

I'll never forget the way he said it. Like he'd choked on his words halfway, swallowed them down and then threw them back up. It stings.

Everyone is quiet. He stares at me.

"You're kidding." He looks around the room wildly.

Tears sputter out of my eyes and drip off my nose. My parents continue to talk but my ears refuse to take it in. I remember him staring at me like a stranger. The inside of my brain rings like I've been struck by lightning.

I become overwhelmed by the almost definite probability that there is no chance of getting back the relationship that I used to have with him. He'll never see me the same or gossip like an elementary schooler at the sight of my hopeless older brother. We'll never have those moments when we look across the room at each other and half roll our eyes when we hear Matt and Elle fighting about her laptop. And what about the ferry? What about watching foreign movies together or those multitudes of television shows we still have yet to finish? I have to leave, I have to leave, I have to leave.

I run up the stairs; my lungs refuse to take rhythmic breaths. Curling up in the corner of my bed, I cry. What am I doing? I'm worthless, stupid, pathetic, trash.

A picture of my dad holding me after I'd just been born hangs on the wall in front of me. His face is open and vulnerable.

Staring at it with swollen eyes, I fall asleep.

My room is dark. The sound of the fan thumping at the foot of my bed keeps up with the pace of my thoughts. The blanket is pulled up around my head; the condensation of my breaths feather around my cheeks.

I'm pregnant. In nine months I'll have a baby. My relationship with my family will never be the same. Owen will get stressed out every time it cries. I'll be sleep deprived. We'll have to play as adults. I'll have to wipe its ass every time shit shoots out of it. And yet…

Joy nestles in my ribcage. The baby will be half of the person I love the most and half of whoever I am (I know, I know, clichéd beyond belief but true nonetheless).

This bundle of love will give me something that I can't begin to describe. Like when you go out of state the first time and see massive empty plains of grass or hills with patches of trees, or even a cloud that's drifting past—which seems insignificant but in your heart you know it's different—you feel new, precious. No, it's not lavish or incredibly interesting, the experience is a swell of a heartbeat. Something that's just... there. And you cradle it in the folds of your brain, but it's meaningful.

While my dad is thinking that this is the end of the world, I can't help but feel like it's the beginning of mine.

"Just relax, okay?" The doctor squirts blue syrup on my pelvis.

I'm six weeks along and they are giving me the first picture of Soybean. Owen and I started calling it that after *The Office* said it in an episode.

My mom stands in the corner, her eyes probing the monitor. She seems happy, but perhaps my excitement is impairing better judgment. Oh well.

Blobs of black shutter to life, squirming around with every movement of the wand. It takes a few moments to get a clear view, then the woman says, "Here it is, you can see her heartbeat. The next time you come, we'll let you hear it."

I know she said 'her' because I'd told her earlier that I was hoping for a girl, but hearing her say it makes everything brighter. I watch Soybean shake, my tears causing the world to be clouded by a soft fog.

I head to Owen's that evening and shake the ultrasound picture in front of his face. "Look at Soybean! Isn't she beautiful?"

"If I could tell what that thing was, I'd probably be agreeing with you." He laughs. I watch as he squints at the flimsy photograph.

The night he told his mother, he said she cried and told his aunt and uncle right after he asked her to keep it private. So, when she comes in and holds out her hand to show the picture to them, I'm hesitant.

"Have you thought of any names yet?" she asks. As she says this I grip the bedding. *Don't say it, please don't say it.* "Because I have a few ideas." *Dammit.*

"Oh yeah?"

"I was thinking that if it's a boy you could have the middle name be two names and one of them be William—we started that tradition when Owen was born."

Inappropriate. Do not betray trust and then name my unborn child. Are you kidding?

"Darcy Cobain if it's a girl and Aiden Holmes or Arthur Henry if it's a boy." I steam on a happy face, but by the expression she gives back to me, she knows it's false. Fun fact: Arthur came from the just King of Camelot; Arthur Pendragon, Darcy meant 'dark one' and I've always been infatuated with the idea of Sherlock Holmes. Do I sound like one of those celebrities that name their children something completely horrific? I hope not.

She stares at Owen, her lips forming a small straight line, then leaves with a curt nod.

"Do you think when she –"

"Or he."

"–comes, my dad will be okay with it?" I rub the inside of my palm. It's a blissful fantasy. The fact is, I know he won't be. But my mind has always taken better to a daydream than a harsh slap of ice that is reality. When all is said and done, Owen and I will be left with a small snotty piglet type of human and our families will watch us with teary eyes—and not out of happiness.

"Maybe." Owen's cherub-like features make me not want to look at him and at the same time I can't look away. He's the embodiment of comfort. I need that.

He leafs through a baby book—the fourth one we've read—and points to the picture of a stroller. "Should we get the one that can be formed into a car seat or the one with a basket at the bottom to hold diapers?"

"I don't know what's happening." Tears wheeze out of me as I speak. "It just keeps coming, what do I do? What do I do?"

"What color is it?" Mom places her hand over my shoulders.

"What do you think?" I palm my eyes, stomach twisting, heart beat flying. "It's *bright red.*"

"It's okay." She rubs my back. Normally I shrivel away from any physical contact my family gives me, but I need her here. "I'll call them up and set an appointment for the morning, okay? Just sit tight for the night, maybe it'll clear up."

The next day is smudged.

I hear its heartbeat for the first and last time.

It is slow, too slow, for a developing fetus.

I want to shout and melt into the abyss formerly known as my heart.

My dad comes in, grin cutting through his face. "I heard the news, I'm so sorry." *No you're not.*

Owen cries, every tear a needle plunging into my spine.

The flowers Alison gives me crumple into brown tissues within days.

The blood won't stop. My eyes are so dry they hurt when I blink. Tears have long since passed. Bubbles swirl around in my stomach, a cold blanket of fresh depression wraps around the aching muscles in my shoulders. The doctor says that it is going to die down, but it has been three hours of nonstop emotional turmoil. Mind buzzing to the point of utter exhaustion, my veins burn against my skin as I fall asleep. Soybean is gone.

⁜

"Do any drugs?" the principal, Kathy Clift, asks, the light through the window reflecting off of her pen. My interview to get into Scriber Lake, the 'second chance' high school, was set for today, a week after my miscarriage. The Becca Law pushed me into a corner and I guess this is my only shot.

"No."

"Drink alcohol?"

"No." I notice a bee trapped inside the window. I quietly resist the urge to let it out.

"Involved with any gangs?"

"No."

She scratches on another 'x' and flips the page.

"Are you pregnant?"

My breath catches, tears crowd my eyes.

"No."

⁜

A Note from Emma

I'd like to say things are fine, but are they ever really? I mean, my relationship with my Dad has been… all right. We don't go anywhere together, but we have a mutual understanding. Of what, I have no idea. As long as it keeps the peace, who cares? Mom's been Mom about everything; sensitive with sorrow, humbled by the sheer "could-have" of it, and is still an amazing mother (seriously, everyone should get on her level). Owen has been better; trying to graduate on time at his humdrum school and save half of every paycheck to get us an apartment is quite a load on his shoulders. He, of course, never shows it because he's a wee gent. I've been taking some medication for depression and I guess it's working (depends who you ask). I got into Scriber and they're helping me out with graduating and all of that fun stuff. Oh, and I've devoted myself to writing a book (a trilogy, because, like my mom says, "good things come in threes") called The Shadow Keeper. All in all, let's just say life is holding its breath for me right now.

"The day before me is fraught with God knows what horrors." John Kennedy Toole, A Confederacy of Dunces (Ignatius J. Reilly)
"Man is not made for defeat."—Ernest Hemingway

LIFE CRASH

BREANNA PRATT

"Everything you say will be recorded, is that okay?"

The state patrolman who has just shown up at my house says this more like a statement than a question.

"That's fine," I reply. I'm not nervous. I figure he just has a few questions to ask about the accident I was involved in a week before.

He turns on a tape recorder and reads me my rights. Then he turns to look at me.

"I saw Rachel this morning," he says, staring at me intently. "She is blind in one eye."

His words are like a crushing weight that has just been dropped on me. Rachel is the most beautiful person I know. How could I have done this to her?

"Serious injuries caused by a hit and run are considered a class B felony," the patrolman continues. His voice is stern and threatening, but he wears a half smile, like he's enjoying this. "Now when you go to court, they can give you anywhere from six months to three years."

Shock and panic wash over me. *Three years? How can this be happening to me? I'm only sixteen. How can I be a felon?* I'm not a bad person but I feel like a monster. *Why did I have to drink so much that night? Why did I get behind that wheel?*

⁕

I couldn't hear anything except the ringing in my ears. I lifted my

WE HOPE YOU RISE UP

head from the steering wheel and saw dim red lights shining through the windshield. I glanced over at the passenger seat and saw my friend slumped over, her silhouette lit by taillights from the car in front of me. Her head leaned to the side, the air bags deflated. I looked up and saw a man staring into the car through the passenger seat window, his face blurry.

A jumble of thoughts raced through my head. *What was going on? Who was that man? Why was Rachel slumped over?* Then it hit me. I'd been in a car accident. I must have hit his car.

"Rachel, wake up!" I yelled. "Rachel! Please." Her head lifted ever so slightly "What do I do?" I asked.

"Go to Ashley's," she replied faintly.

I stepped on the gas and the engine roared, but didn't move. I tried again, but nothing happened.

"Rachel, the car won't go." I was drunk, but managed to realize that the car had shifted gears. I put it in drive, pulled out and drove away.

I couldn't see straight; there was two of everything. I closed one eye hoping it would help me focus on which lines divided the lanes. I was worried about Rachel but couldn't concentrate on more than one thing at a time. I came to a stoplight and looked over to check on her. Her eyes were closed and she wasn't moving. I assumed she was unconscious.

"Rachel!" She didn't respond. She was leaning over to the side, with her hair draped over her face.

"Rachel!" I yelled louder, trying to wake her up. Again no response.

The light turned green so I continued driving. I kept yelling her name, begging for her to wake up. Worry stormed through my mind as I drove up Highway 99. I was in shock, but I was also so drunk it was hard to focus.

I stopped at another light and I looked over again at Rachel. I moved her long, tinted red hair out of her face to get a good look at her, but it was too dark to see anything. The light turned green and then I was driving again. I kept yelling her name but she wouldn't respond. I felt my panic rising. I tried to concentrate on my speed. I was going 45 in a 40. I tried not to swerve, and did everything I could to obey the driving laws so I could make it to Ashley's house and get Rachel the help she needed.

I finally arrived at Ashley's townhome parking lot, put the car in park and turned off the engine. I immediately turned to Rachel, continuing to try and wake her up. I finally got a good look at her face. Her eye had red marks on it but I couldn't see it entirely. I don't know how long we sat there before I heard a knock at the driver's side window. I turned to look and saw a cop.

Holy shit. I felt my body tense up and my knees start to shake. *What was he doing there?* I thought I'd gotten away.

"Rachel! Please wake up!" I urged in a hushed panic. I felt scared and alone, even though one of my closest friends was right beside me.

I heard the knocking again and slowly opened my car door.

"How old are you?" the cop asked me.

"Sixteen," I responded in a shaky voice. He looked down at my feet at an empty Olde English can. He shined his flashlight on it.

"Is that yours?" he asked in a stern voice.

"No," I lied.

Do you know how much you've had to drink?"

My head went into a fog as I thought about the forty-ounce beer I had just downed.

"I don't know exactly," I mumbled.

The cop walked away to speak with a female officer. I shook Rachel slightly.

"Dude, there's cops. You need to wake up," I pleaded. She was twenty-one, five years older than me. I figured she'd know what to do.

Rachel took a breath and brought her hands to her face. Then she started crying. "My face hurts," she moaned.

I heard the cop back at the car door. "License and registration," he demanded. I immediately turned back to Rachel because it was her Hyundai Elantra. Crying, she pointed to her glove box. I opened it and frantically started pulling out every paper in there, handing it all to the cop. He left to converse with the other officers.

"Hey, look," I said in a comforting tone. "Everything will be okay, okay?" Rachel didn't respond.

"I swear you'll be okay. It's me who's fucked. You're definitely okay."

The cop came back and ordered me to get out of the car.

"I love you Rachel" I said before following his command. "Everything will be all right. I promise."

The officer led me to a line that divided the parking spaces. I had to pee so badly, but I knew the cop wouldn't let me. It was unbearable so I started to pee myself right there. I looked around and saw a fire truck, an ambulance, and about eight cop cars surrounding me. Red and blue lights lit up the street and bounced off the townhouse's walls. I looked the other direction and saw a lady cop. My eyes locked on Ashley and her mom, Lucy, standing ten yards behind her.

"Is that Breanna?" I heard Lucy yell. Heat crept up my face because I knew they were watching me fail at my attempt to walk in a straight line. The cop put handcuffs tightly around my wrists and forcefully guided me to a police car. I knew at this point I was screwed. I wasn't scared; I just wished I knew what the outcome would be.

I saw a stretcher being rushed out of an ambulance and realized it was for Rachel. I was worried but I knew they would take care of her.

"I love you," I heard Ashley yell as I was put into the back of the cop car. But I didn't get the chance to say anything back because the door was shut behind me.

My arrival at Denney an hour later was a blur. My head was spinning and I was still so drunk I could hardly walk. I was bombarded with questions and then directed to a spot by the wall.

"Put your hands on the wall and spread your legs," a woman police officer ordered. I did as I was told and she began patting me down. My jeans were soaked with pee and when she got to my legs, I felt her pause. I looked back at her and saw her face contorted in disgust.

The woman walked me to a bathroom with a toilet and shower stall. There were no doors or curtains on the shower—just a drain in the center of the floor to catch the water. She handed me two mouthwash-sized paper cups: one containing shampoo, the other body wash.

"Take your clothes off and leave them there," she said, pointing to a shelf on the wall that opened to a cubby window. I noticed that the shelf contained a basket holding an orange jumpsuit, grandma-looking white underwear and a pair of tall, orange socks.

"And put those on when you are done showering," she added, motioning to the clothes.

"When you're done, knock on the door and we'll come let you out," she said before leaving the room.

I looked at the door and realized there was no doorknob. Normally my claustrophobia would kick in and crushing anxiety would take over. But thankfully I was too drunk to care. Exhaustion slammed into me. All I wanted was sleep. I took a quick rinse in the cold shower, put on the orange jumpsuit and pounded on the door.

Moments later, I was lying on a mattress on a cement floor in a holding cell and heard the steel door slam behind me. I closed my eyes, hoping sleep would bring an end to my nightmare.

The patrolman is staring at me and his words are still screaming in my mind. *Rachel blind in one eye. Three years locked away.*

Then he speaks again, delivering the next blow. "You hit a car with two little girls in it."

My heart drops. I'm not ready for more bad news. *What? Are they blind too?* I sarcastically think to myself.

I don't say anything, but tears pour out of my eyes. I haven't cried once during this entire situation. But hearing about Rachel, the possibility of three years doing time and now these two little girls. It's too much. I feel like I've messed up my entire life. *How will I get a job in the future? A felon?*

"They're perfectly fine," the state patrolman says, interrupting my thoughts. For a second relief washes over me, then despair sets in again.

"Now that I'm done talking, why don't you go ahead and state your story," he says.

I can't breathe. I feel hot and overwhelmed.

"Um, I don't want to say anything before talking to my lawyer," I finally say.

I see nothing but disdain in the patrolman's eyes as I walk him to the door.

I slam it closed behind him, feeling like I've just slammed the door to my future.

A Note from Breanna

Though it took some time to heal, Rachel eventually regained her eyesight completely. It's been nearly five months since the crash and

I've been more responsible with my decisions. I got a job and haven't driven or had anything to drink since the incident. I was charged with a DUI, MIP, Vehicle Assault, and a Hit and Run and was fined $2,000 in tickets. Court is pending. The crash has taught me a few valuable life lessons: not to drink and drive, and to not to take anything or anyone for granted. I am now a junior at Scriber. After graduation, I hope to become psychologist and use my experiences to help others.

"For every dark night there's a brighter day."—Tupac

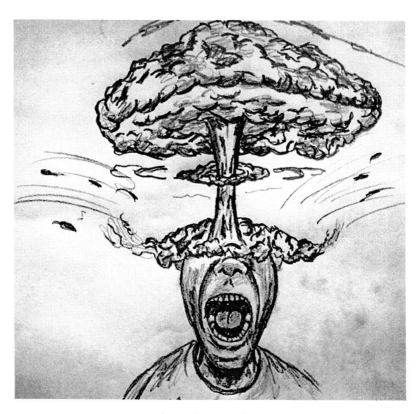

Artist: Breanna Pratt

ASCENSION

CYRENA FULTON

I lay on my rock-hard bed, staring at the Bucky board under the mattress above me. I smile contentedly at the silence, the peace, the fact that I'm finally *free*.

The windows at my feet, head, and left side are all covered, leaving me in near darkness, despite the bright sunshine penetrating the glass on the other side of the sixteen-by-eight foot travel trailer. The fake blonde wood paneling glows at the touch of filtered light in the places it can reach. Though it is underlit, I can still see the picture of Ben Drowned and the Neff smiley face logo stuck to the bottom of my sister's bed. The minimal decoration is accented by decade-old graffiti, produced by the hands of toddlers. The writing brings me back.

I'd made him angry. I don't know how, but I—a three year old—had made him angry enough to punish me. His large hands picked me up from the playpen and bent me over his knee. The sound of a few loud slaps resonated off the unfinished plywood walls of the basement computer room, followed by a sting in my rear. I wailed at the pain as he put me back in the playpen. Before his arms retreated, my father picked up my one-year-old sister from where she sat next to me and turned toward the wooden door. I stood and watched, clutching the top bar of the playpen as his short, dark hair disappeared. He turned out the lights and closed the door behind him, leaving me in complete darkness. Not a word was said, no look taken back at me. I listened through my desperate cries as he climbed the stairs to the main floor of my grandparents' house, the wood sagging and groaning under his weight. My sobs grew louder, more persistent. The dark was scary and I was alone. I could taste blood from all the screaming. I just yelled for my mommy over and over again until my throat hurt too much to even whimper, but she never came. I lay down and silently sobbed, cold and stranded.

I shift on my bed, searching for a more comfortable position. I am once again in the safety of the travel trailer. I look around at my surroundings, the feeling of calm settling over me. *You're no longer there. No need to fret over something you don't have any control over. At least he's gone now.* The silence envelops me in its embrace. I breathe a sigh of relief as my thoughts jump to the nightmare of the house I stayed in last.

She screamed at me in that shrill voice of hers, imitating nails on a chalkboard. It was just like any other given day, a screaming match between the two of us, a twelve year-old versus a forty-something. Bridget had had it out for me ever since we'd moved in with her and her three children; I hadn't a shred of an idea why. The grey carpeting sank under her immense weight, creaking and moaning. She shook her stumpy fists in my face, long manicured nails digging into her plump palm. The bangles on her wrist jingled, stirring the dust in the air. As she approached me, I looked at the stationary wind chime that hung on the inside of the small picture window to our right, giving the illusion of peace, happiness. She stepped closer, invading my personal space. A sickly sweet perfume tangled with her bad breath. My blood boiled.

"Don't glare at me!" she yelled. There it was—the usual accusation.

"I'm not glaring!" The same response as the last few hundred times crossed my lips.

Lightning-quick, her hand connected with my face. She'd never hit me before. I stood in shocked silence, frozen by fear and hurt. My eyes brimmed with tears. *Why?*

⚜

I smile, inhaling the sweet scent of autonomy as I bury my head in my pillow. Happiness rushes through me; it makes me feel so light. The small space heater at the other end of the trailer buzzes to life, adding to the warmth of my delight. This place where I sleep, where I dream, is my little slice of the proverbial 'Heaven'.

⚜

Another night, another battle of the voices. This time the fight was between Bridget and her youngest daughter, Shannon. I don't remember what the argument was about, probably something stupid. Shannon's fiery red hair bounced with the indignant bob of her head, temper flaring, which just so happened to be as fiery as her hair. Her freckly Barbie face contorted into an ugly mask of rage.

All of a sudden, Shannon ran to the kitchen. I could hear metal being pulled from wood. The pretentious way she held the steak knife to her own temple, right hand gripping the black plastic handle, gave not even a twitch of the self-fear I knew must have been there. Her mother sat in horrified awe in front of the fireplace, her large frame over-filling the child-sized Raggedy Anne chair. My eyes widened, blood running ice cold, pounding in my ears like a locomotive. My mother also witnessed the unfolding commotion. The screaming once again resumed.

"Go to bed," she ordered my sister and me. There was so much urgency in her voice and in the situation. The screaming, oh god the *screaming*, continued until the police arrived. I heard the hammer of footsteps race through the house. I heard the thump of a body hitting the stairs. I heard the metallic clicks of handcuffs. I heard the crying. I heard the front door open and close. Then I heard the silence.

⚜

I open my eyes, staring at the ruined cardboard lining the bunk overhead. *It's over.* After ten years of living in daily misery, we were finally evicted from that house and split from the other family. My mom, sister, and I are now living on the side of my mom's parents' house in a travel trailer. Though it's not ideal, still not where I want to be, I'll get there. For now, I'm finally content with life, finally untethered from the constant pain and fear. I rise from my bed, ready to deal with this newest chapter, ready to ascend.

⚜

Note from Cyrena

Things have gotten better for me, although they're still not ideal. I still live in the tiny trailer, sharing the space with my mother, sister, and medium-sized dog. It's cramped and emotions run high quite often, but it is so much better. As of late my mother has been talking about moving back in with them. I'm avidly and openly against the idea, but we'll probably end up doing it anyway. I've been with my boyfriend for over a year now and he makes everything bearable. I'm sixteen and a sophomore in high school. My goal at this point is to graduate on time with all A's, get married, and move. I hope to either become a touring musician or a novelist while working a side job.

"If it doesn't challenge you, it won't change you"—Fred DeVito

GONE

KAI LEE

I join the sea of sixth graders migrating out of the two small doors at the end of school. As I'm walking along the parking lot, I see my mom's Kia Rondo and stop in my tracks. I only live a block away. Why is she here?

A rush of excited energy takes over me as I walk up to the car, racking my brain for reasons she would decide to pick me up at school.

"What's up?" I ask her cheerfully as I get in the car.

"We're going to Grandma's," she says with one of her forced smiles.

I feel my excitement leave. It's just the usual: she and dad must have had another fight. I'm still happy to see her, though, because I haven't seen her since the night before because she leaves for work so early. I'm also a little bit curious about what happened.

We crawl towards the train of cars pulling out of the school parking lot. I casually lean back into my seat and put in my favorite CD, ready for the hour-long drive to Duvall where my grandmother lives. But instead of heading to the highway, my mom pulls into Game Stop. Now I'm really confused. My mind is in a scramble.

"What are we doing?" I ask.

"We're moving in with Grandma and your dad has your Xbox."

Of course he does.

My anger slowly rises as I remember coming home a few days before to see cords hanging limply where my Xbox should have been. He probably has it hidden in his closet again.

"We're not going back to get it," Mom says sternly.

With that statement, my suspicions are confirmed. I feel relief and happiness wash over me. We won't live through that nightmare anymore. I smile as I picture myself in what's going to be my new room. I look out the window, visualizing myself relaxing in my permanent room at Grandma's—a room bigger, cleaner, nicer than my own.

My mom sighs as we walk into the store. I can't tell if it's her dislike for the store or the events of today. We head toward the cashier and I ask for an Xbox. She hands the cashier $250 as I rhythmically tap my fingers on the counter. Now I know she's serious. We're low on money and this isn't something my mom would do if we were going home any time soon. I smile to myself as we leave the store, happy that my new Xbox is the Elite version. But I'm also thinking of all the work I'm going to have to re-do to get to where I was in my game.

We start driving again and my thoughts drift to my life. I roll my eyes as I think about trading my dad's craziness for my grandma's craziness. But Grandma's is pure cluelessness while my dad's is manipulation and rage. A familiar surge of anger shoots through me as my thoughts jump back to the morning's disaster.

"Wake the fuck up!"

My dad's words echoed in my head but I couldn't tell if it was a dream or real. My head was swimming; I was in such a deep sleep that I felt like I was rising from the dead. I heard my bedroom door slam and it jolted me awake.

It was real.

My dad's bipolar personality meant that sometimes he was my best friend and other times he was a hypocritical asshole who blamed everything on everyone else.

This morning it was clear his asshole personality had taken over.

Of course, I thought as I slowly pulled myself out of bed. It was crappy, but I was used to it.

I walked down the hall like a zombie. My mind was in a fog. *What day is it? What are we doing at school today? Is Mom home?*

I stumbled into the bathroom and played with the knobs on the shower faucet until it was the temperature I wanted it. I heard the familiar hissing sound as the water spurted out and stood there for a few seconds with my eyes closed, trying to relax as the water washed over me and my mind finally caught up with the rest of my body.

It's Tuesday...I'm just going to the music room.

"Shit," I said, suddenly remembering my unpleasant wake up a few minutes earlier. *Mom must be at work.*

My dad's door creaked open and I heard him shuffle his way down the hall towards the kitchen. I felt the familiar dread because I knew he was up to his usual morning routine. I tried to distract myself as I heard the beer can pop open. He always drank more when he was really mad.

You're such a low-life, drinking at seven in the morning.

I took a deep breath and pushed my feelings to one side, knowing that I would be out the door soon and I wouldn't have to deal with him. I had become really good at blocking out my emotions. I forced myself out of the shower and headed to my room to find something to wear. I hated dealing with my dad's problems, but I hated school more. Since the second grade, I had been getting suspended or sent to the office pretty much every day, so school for me was about as fun as prison.

When I got in trouble for talking too much, for talking back, for moving around too much or for throwing eraser caps, I was usually sent to in-school suspension. I would sit in a dark room with one small light bulb with nothing to do except stare out a small window into the parking lot. Sometimes I would sit there all day and my friends wouldn't even know I was at school until I got out for lunch. I would get some minor relief standing in the lunch line before going back into solitary confinement. There was no point for me to even try at school.

I finally got my clothes on and headed to the kitchen for a ham and cheese Hot Pocket. I put it in the microwave and set it for two minutes. While it was cooking, I went to grab a paper plate but accidently knocked a small box of plastic spoons off the table. I heard them crash to the ground and knew what was going to happen next.

"Shit," I whispered under my breath.

"WHAT THE HELL ARE YOU DOING?" my dad yelled from his room.

"Noooothing."

"Well that was something," he barked back.

I heard the bed creak and knew he was coming to investigate. I prepared myself for the yelling. I picked up the two spoons that had fallen out of the box and threw them away. I quickly glanced at the microwave to see how much time was left. One minute, 27 seconds.

What can I do instead of stand here and listen to him rant and rave?

I put my hand on my hair and realized I forgot to brush it down after drying it so it was sticking up. Just as I was about to turn around to head back to the bathroom, I smelled his presence—old beer and sweat. The stench made me hold my breath.

He barreled around the corner, his greenish brown eyes searching the ground, ready to explode. His face was contorted in anger, making the scars from his childhood dog attack come alive. His long, wavy hair made him look like a crazed Medusa, with shoulder-length strands going in every direction.

"What the fuck are you doing in here?" he demanded. His voice was loud but not quite a yell.

"Nothing," I said quietly, my head dropping. "A few spoons fell and I threw them away."

"Why would you waste things like that?" he demanded, raising his tone. He always blew up over little things.

Here we go.

After years of hearing his yelling, I had gotten pretty good at blocking out noise. That was all it was, noise. I slipped past him and walked down the hall to the bathroom. I looked at myself in the mirror and saw that the hair on the back of my head was standing up like the main character from the Little Rascals.

Then he was at the door. "Don't turn your fucking back on me when I'm talking to you!" he yelled.

I didn't reply. I just stood there trying to pat my hair down. *Beep beep beep.* I heard the microwave go off and my stomach growled at the sound. I took one last look in the mirror and thought, *fuck it*. My dad was still standing in the doorway saying something about how I was going to get beat up or killed by someone in the real world if I treated them the same way I treated him. He always had something to say about everything as long as it was how the other person was wrong and he was right.

"Well, hopefully people won't go on yelling about two spoons that fell," I mumbled as I walked past him. I knew that nothing good was going to come out of snapping back, but I felt happier saying my clever comment than just thinking it.

"YOU FUCKING SMARTASS! YOUR MOM BETTER DEAL WITH YOU BEFORE I DO!" he screamed. The threats came often but I was still scared of what he might do. The thought of me and him going at it made adrenaline pulse through my veins. I couldn't fight back—my little eleven year-old body would be crushed in a second. My dad looked fat but was actually well built.

I went into the kitchen and tore off a piece of paper towel to wrap my Hot Pocket. I had planned on sitting down to watch TV, but I knew I wouldn't even be able to hear it over his yelling and I wanted to be as far away from him as possible. Instead, I wrapped it up and walked out into the living room. All I heard was noise as I tried to block him out again. *That's all it is... noise* I repeated to myself.

I wanted to leave as soon as I could, but I couldn't find my backpack. I waited for a pause in his ranting. The air was thick and hot with anger.

"Wh-Where's my backpack?" I stammered, cutting him off—a bad idea. I took a quick glance at his face and saw his tight-lipped, red face with a vein bulging out on his forehead. There was no color in his dark, demented eyes. I found my backpack but it was on a chair covered in coats. The only problem was that it sat right next to where my dad was standing.

His eyes followed my eyes, and in an instant it was flying at me. I didn't react quickly enough and it hit me in the face. There was nothing to do but leave. I was too stunned to feel pain, but my face felt so hot I thought it might melt off. I tasted blood. He just stood there and watched as I calmly picked up my backpack and left without saying a word.

Even though I go to my grandma's all the time, I feel a rush of excitement and happiness as we start heading down the hill to her house. My grandma keeps everything around her house really nice, but today—knowing that this is my house now—it looks even nicer. I feel the stress leave my body.

"We live here now," I tell her when she meets us at the door.

She smiles. "Good."

A Note from Kai

At the end of the school year we moved back with my dad. He was calm for a little while, but soon went back to his old ways. Even though life is back to the way it was, I'm happier than I was in the 6th grade. I'm doing so much better in school now. Scriber has given me another chance and my grades are proof; I will finish my sophomore year with all required credits. My dream is to get a business degree and own a restaurant. My mom tells me that if I focus on all the bad things in life, that's all I will see, so with that in mind I choose to live life happily.

"Hope is not dead, it is just larger than our imaginations; its purpose extending far beyond our comprehension."—Anonymous

SEEMS LIKE EVERY GIRL HAS DADDY ISSUES

HAYLEE PEARSON

I stare at the screen, feeling my stomach sink to my feet—then to the floor.

I whimper slightly and my boyfriend, Jake, looks over from the other side of the couch. I'm shaking as I hand the iPad to him. He reads, then hands it back and I see my father's gruesome face again.

CALIFORNIA HIGHWAY PATROL CHASES GOLF CART ON FREEWAY AT 10 MPH, the headline reads.

I can't help myself; I continue reading. *In the early morning of October 24th, 2014, 35-year-old Cory Pearson, a post-release community supervision parolee, reportedly stole a golf cart from the Sun Valley Bulb Farm in Arcata. Pearson, while under the influence of methamphetamine, was driving the stolen golf cart on Lamphere Road in Arcata.* Sweat coats my hands and dread slithers up my throat as I fight back years of memories that have been locked away for too long.

❋

The front door opened and then slammed shut. I cowered in the corner of my room, frozen; I knew my dad was home, most likely drunk and angry. Confirmation of that came as he began to slur words at my mom. I turned off my light, then pressed myself to the back of my bed, hoping he wouldn't be able to see me. My parents screamed, stomped and threw objects for what seemed like hours.

"Haylee! Quick, get in the car!" my mom yelled as she ran into her room. I heard the car keys clink together. My father was close behind her, still slurring. One command I understood from him:

"Haylee, don't you *dare* leave that room!"

I heard something being thrown and then my father screaming. "SHE'S EIGHT, SAM. SHE WILL NOT MOVE A GODDAMN MUSCLE!"

His voice paralyzed me. I grabbed my brown blanket and my stuffed pink and blue beaver, Chewie, and crawled to the door.

As I slipped my shoes on, I heard a crash and a thud from the hallway. I peeked out, my body tense and shaking, and saw my mom on the ground with their TV inches from her back, shattered on the ground.

I ran to the door that led into the garage, jumped into our dark blue Mustang and locked the door. My mom jumped in moments later, locked her door, and scrambled for the key. We both saw my father appear in the doorway. His neck was thick with rage and there was fire in his eyes. As my mom turned the key and revved the engine, he grabbed a hammer from the table and smashed in the window on my mother's side. Glass shattered as my father screamed words that sounded like a different language.

I smelled the stale beer and cigarettes on his breath through the broken window and cringed. I hated that familiar smell. My mom backed up a bit more, so he ran to the back of the car.

"Ruhn me ovah, Sam, do it. *Do it!*" he challenged.

Everything in me went numb. My mom maneuvered around him and drove away. We drove for what seemed like an hour in tense silence until finally pulling in to a McDonald's.

"I left my money, phone and wallet at the house," she said. "Our options are now extremely limited. We can wait until we think he has left or we can call the police."

An old pay phone stood in front of us. I weighed the consequences of each before voting for the latter. "He doesn't get to get away with this again," I said. "It's out of hand. Call the police." She stepped out of the car to the phone and I noticed a large, purple-and-blue bruise peeking out from under her shirt. On the way home, I dozed off with the blanket wrapped around me, cuddling Chewie.

I woke up to police lights surrounding our house. I headed inside, climbed into my mom's bed and watched TV as she spoke to the officers. Eventually she came in and lay next to me.

A few hours later I woke up to the sound of the living room TV, footsteps, and mumbling. I hobbled out of bed and walked down the hall to check things out. My dad's head poked up from the couch. He was cuddling our Rottweiler, C.J.

"Poor Ceejers, had to deal with cops in his yard. Mommy called the cops on us, C.J." he mumbled, coming down from his drunken night.

"How did you get out, Daddy?" I asked.

"I ran through the back yard and climbed over the fence, baby girl. Your daddy's got skills."

He reeked of alcohol. I curled up onto the floor by the couch and watched TV after he passed out, overwhelmed with hopelessness and regret.

I woke the next morning to the sounds of the TV blaring and my father snoring on the couch behind me. When I turned the TV off, the absence of sound startled him. He sat up and stared at me with blank eyes.

"Daddy, do you remember what happened last night?" I asked him. The smell of morning breath and booze coated the air around us. He yawned.

"No, Angel, what happened?"

Without answering, I stood up and went into the kitchen. I looked out the sliding glass door to the backyard. The small playhouse replicated a real house, with a white deck and front door, adjustable glass windows, black tiled roof and sunny yellow paint on the outside.

Such a perfect house. I wanted to live there.

❖

A blurry video plays on the iPad: a white golf cart and three police SUV's chasing after it. The video is such low-quality I can't see my father at all, just the golf cart he's driving. But the photo of his mug shot stares back at me. His eyes look black and hollowed-out from the inside and he's smiling like a five-year-old who loves being in trouble. The red scabs on his face show the years that meth has held him in her claws. I don't recognize the person who is supposed to be my father.

Jake wraps his arms around me, kisses my forehead and holds me.

❖

My father's eyes blinked open. The stench from his urine and excrement bags crept into my nose, poorly masked by antiseptic and rubbing alcohol.

I did my best not to tear up in front of him, but he was hooked up to so many tubes. His skin was pale, cold and bluish. His normally dark blue eyes were blemished with blood spots.

When he noticed the tubes he thrashed around, trying to pull them out. After the nurse asked him to stop, he shook the bed. A bald, goateed doctor entered the room and looked down at my dad.

"Do you know who you are?" he asked.

My father turned toward him and began talking like he was an actor scripting his lines. "My name is Cory Pearson. I am thirty-three years old."

"What's the year?"

"May...no, no, no, June, 2013?" He looked up like a child asking a teacher if his answer is correct.

It was July.

I choked up. He didn't remember anything about this last month, or me. After three years of hardly any contact except for the occasional phone call and prison letters, he didn't remember anything. Nothing.

I was sixteen years old, in Nevada for about three weeks with my father's mom, her son (my Uncle Spencer) and their dog, Bodie. The trip was mainly to see my dad, but that was before he relapsed the first week of my visit. My grandmother banned him from seeing me after that. She locked all the computers and wouldn't let me call him. He had dragged her down this road so many times, she claimed, that she was protecting me from what he'd put her through.

I bit my tongue and focused on what the doctor was saying. In order not to cry, I reached into my bag and found Chewie. My dad always teased me about having such a connection to a stuffed animal, but he did, too. I sat Chewie next to my dad's hand and backed away, hoping for some kind of recognition.

"Cory, do you know what happened to you?" one of the nurses asked.

I knew. My dad had tried to kill himself; this was the ninth attempt. The doctor droned on with details I had heard many times during the past four days. He had jumped off a cliff into Lake Tahoe. He had been high on meth for seven days. When he jumped, a family on a boat saw him and called 911. During the rescue he went into cardiac arrest. When they revived him, they drove him to the hospital where doctors gave him a 0.1% chance of survival and flew him to another facility.

My dad looked blankly around at the nurses. Then he spotted Chewie. His eyes went dark and his aura began to fall. Our eyes locked and I tried to smile. He picked up Chewie and threw him into the garbage can.

He grasped at his IV, screaming and cursing at the nurses. I grabbed Chewie out of the garbage, put him in my bag and left. My oh-so-wonderful father was alive and I didn't expect anything else from him.

I walked through the white doors, down the lobby and into the garden. I found a bush that was hollow but thick, and wiggled my way in. I sat on top of a flat plastic electric generator cover and cried until every muscle in my body stopped shaking. I held Chewie for safety and focused on my breathing, inhaling the scent of the lavender bush next to me and staring at the abstract canvas of the orange, pink, yellow and red sky.

After calling my mom and arranging my trip back to Seattle, I worked my way back to my father's room and found him alone, sleeping. I sat next to the bed, holding his hand, remembering the conversations and adventures we had shared less than a month before.

One night in particular stood out from our five good days together. We were sitting out in front of my grandmother's house at midnight, staring at the blue moon, talking about everything good and bad—our past, his future, my future.

"Dad, do you remember the day I told you I saw colors around people? Auras?" I asked, feeling so warm and close.

"No, Angel. You told me that? It makes sense. I have always known you were going to do beautiful things. I always knew you were different," he said.

Such a different response from the last time we'd discussed the topic, when he had told me, "Haylee, if you ever tell anyone you see colors on people, they will call you a fucking freak."

The strong smell of antiseptic brought me back. I noticed his bags were no longer filled with blood. His eyes fluttered and he squeezed my hand as his eyes scrunched up and he yawned. He looked at me and smiled.

A nurse came in, took his blood, adjusted his tubes and gave him new bags.

"Do you remember who this is, Cory?" she asked. I looked up at her in confusion. "He's been forgetting everything every time he wakes up, darling."

"Of course. This is my little girl," he replied, but then asked, "When did you come, Shorty?"

I smiled at the nickname. "I came here about a month ago, Daddy, but I'm leaving on Monday."

He nodded and turned his head toward mine. I kissed his cheek before grabbing my jacket and wrapping it up like a pillow. I laid my head down next to his and placed Chewie on his lap. This time he grabbed Chewie and wrapped him up like a child.

I grabbed his hand, feeling relieved. After the nurse left I heard some other nurses outside of the room talking.

"His daughter's in there," one of them said.

"This family has a lot of issues," the other one replied. "Seems like every girl has daddy issues these days." They continued their conversation as they headed down the hall.

Despite her comments and so many days of panic and anxiety, knowing my dad was alive and here with me brought a sense of peace.

Despite all my daddy issues.

"Talk to me, babe, "Jake says, look over at me. "Tell me what you're thinking."

"I should hate him," I say, hearing all of the voices inside me telling me to drop him. "But he's my dad."

Jake is familiar with my ongoing state of confusion.

"For six years he's been in and out of jail and rehab," I continue. "He's told so many lies, broken so many promises."

Jake listens to the rest of my rant and is quiet for a few seconds. I can tell he's thinking it through.

"Babe, you know what you need to do," he says finally. "Write about it. How he chooses to respond to your view of the situation is the answer to how your relationship with him will go."

I nod. I hate addiction and what it has turned him into. *Flashed Junk Mind* by Milky Chance plays on the Xbox as I agree to the answer Jake has come up with.

I have to write this all out. To untangle the knots in my brain, I need to write this out.

A Note from Haylee

Every day, step by step, I sort through the tangled knots in my brain—the anxiety, the mental illness. I have accepted that I needed to go through these events for a reason. Without them, I wouldn't be able to wake up to the love of my life, Jake, every morning. I wouldn't be the considerate and caring person I am today if had stayed with my father when my parents divorced. If I was not meant to be okay, all of the traumas I have experienced would have killed me. I can never take any of the events back, so I'm choosing to be grateful instead. I wrote this story because I needed a conclusion for myself, but if it helps anyone, the struggle of writing this will be even more worthwhile.

"My soul honors your soul. I honor the place where the entire universe resides. I honor the light, love, truth, beauty & peace within you, because it is also within me. We are one, Namaste."

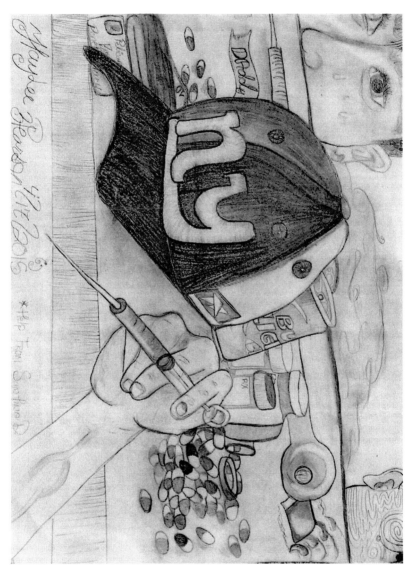

Artist: Haylee Pearson

LOOKING THROUGH THE GLASS

ISABEL CORDOVA

"Mi amor. We're going to go see your dad. Go get ready," my mom says.

"Are you serious?" I scream with excitement. I rush to put on my puffy, pink dress, then ask my mom to brush and do my hair. She's surprised. I'd usually rather wear jeans and a t-shirt and wear my hair down. My dad always backs me up and tells my mom he loves my casual look and my curly, messy hair. But my mom doesn't think it's an appropriate look for a seven year-old girl. I know dressing up makes my mom happy, and I want to make her happy so she will take me to my dad as quickly as possible.

As soon as I'm ready, we get in the car with a family friend who calls himself an attorney. I have no idea what that means. He and my mom start to have an adult conversation that I don't bother to pay attention to. All I can think about is my dad. It feels like the car is crawling and I just want to speed it up so I can get to him as quickly as possible. My mind is a jumble of thoughts. *Where has my dad been? Are we going to go see him at his new work? Is that what's been keeping him away from me for the past week?*

I can't wait to show my dad my pink dress and tell him I let Mom do my hair. I want him to know that I have been behaving.

After what feels like hours, we finally arrive at a big, brown building. There are so many walls surrounding the building that it looks like a fortress. I'm confused. This is definitely not an office building. I can't really tell where I am. I see police officers surrounding the building and cop cars in the parking lot.

"Ma, where is my dad?" I ask. "Why are there so many policemen and police cars?"

My mom looks scared, which makes me even more confused.

"Be quiet or you won't be able to see him," she says in a serious voice. I need to see my dad so I don't say another word.

I follow my mom and her attorney friend into the building. There's a check-in area in the front. My mom's friend talks to a police officer. Then we're taken to a room full of chairs. All I can see are more police officers, a lot of white women in heels and skirts, and men in suits carrying papers and bags. Nobody looks like my family.

"We need to wait here until it's our visiting time," my mom whispers, motioning for me to take a seat on one of the chairs.

What does she mean, "visiting time"? I want to scream at her and tell her to take me to see my dad. But I don't say anything because I don't want to risk missing my chance.

I follow her and take a seat on one of the plastic chairs. While we wait, I start thinking about the last time I saw my dad. My parents had been arguing for hours and my mom was in tears. I could still hear her voice in my mind.

"You are hurting me! Let go of me!"

It scared me when my parents fought because my dad had a bad temper and I never knew what he would do. That night I was hiding in my room. I could hear Mom begging Dad to let go of her hair, but he wouldn't.

"Shut the fuck up!" I heard him shout at her. "You shouldn't have pissed me off!"

I had felt my stomach tense and the familiar fear washed over me. I stayed hidden in my room, trying to block out the yelling and crying and my dad's angry voice. My room was the only place I felt safe.

The yelling and banging suddenly stopped, followed by a voice I had never heard before. It was a man's voice. It was deep and loud, and he was speaking English.

I curled up in a ball and covered my ears. After a few minutes my mom stepped into my room. I uncovered my ears and looked up at her. Her eyes were red and the front part of her head had bloody bald spots. The ponytail she always styled so perfectly was halfway undone. My eyes locked on her face. It was covered in bruises and blood.

Tears rushed down my face. I jumped to my feet and ran to give her a hug.

"Are you okay, Ma?" I asked. Her bruises and cuts looked so bad. "Where's Dad?"

It was so quiet in the house. Not hearing his voice was eerie. My mom was silent for a minute before answering.

"He's not here," she said finally. "He's gone for a while."

"It's time for your visit with Francisco Cordova," an officer says sternly.

I jump out of my chair. My feet just want to rush to my dad. We follow the police officer through a grey, metal door. A big smile breaks open across my face the minute I see him. He's sitting behind a scratched-up glass wall with a phone in his hand, ready to talk to us.

I hesitate and stare at him. *Why is he behind the glass wall? And why is he holding a phone?* He looks like he hasn't slept in days. His curly messy hair only makes him look worse. I feel scared, but am anxious to talk to him.

My mom speaks to him first. Finally it's my turn. I grab the receiver from my mom.

"Papi!" I shout into the phone.

"Have you been behaving, my princess?" he asks. As soon as he speaks he starts to cry.

"Yes, Yes! I have been listening to Mom," I reply. Seeing him cry makes me cry, too.

"Very good, my princess. Keep obeying to your mother." He's crying harder, wiping away his tears.

"I will for you, Papi. But look at what Mom bought me." I climb onto a chair by the window so he can see my pink, puffy dress.

"You look like a princess," he says, avoiding my eyes.

"Can I hug you?" I plead. "Papi, I want to hug and kiss you!"

He remains silent and just stares at me.

"Dad, come out!" I shout. I feel my body start to shake. *Why is he in there behind that glass?* My thoughts begin to race. *Is this my fault? Maybe if I behaved better he would come home again. Maybe if I stopped crying...* but I can't stop.

The police officer comes back into the room.

"Keep your daughter calm or you'll have to leave," he orders my mom.

She nods and tells me to calm down and stop crying. But I can't. I'm too upset. My dad has always told me that if you don't obey the law you'll go to prison. Maybe even be sent back to Mexico, where both my parents are from. I may only be a seven year-old, but all of a sudden, everything is starting to make sense to me. I realize where my dad is and why he's behind the glass wall. Suddenly I wonder if I'll ever be able to hug him again.

"I'll be home soon, princess," he tries to assure me. "I just have to finish some things here and I'll be with you as soon as I can."

"You promise?" I sob into the phone. "Please, promise me, Daddy!"

"I promise you Isa..." he whispers, calling me by his special nickname for me. He stands and hangs up the phone. He looks at me through tears, turns and walks away. My stomach drops when I see him turn his back on me.

I can't leave him in this place. I have to rescue him. I want to go behind the glass, grab him by his hand and take him home with me. I'm daddy's little girl. How can he just walk away and abandon me?

"It's time to go home," I hear my mom say. I feel her dragging me away from the scratched-up glass window. I try to fight her off and look through the window one last time, hoping my dad will come back.

But he's gone.

A Note from Isabel

My dad was deported to Mexico a few weeks after my visit. But like he promised, he came back home a couple of months later. He has been suffering with his own addictions and anger problems throughout my entire life. I'm not daddy's little girl anymore, but I've learned to forgive and love my father because I know he also has a story and a struggle. I'm currently 18 years old. I'm a senior at Scriber and I'm working hard to graduate by next year or before. After graduation, I'm going to become a social worker and help children find their voice and power, just like I did through writing.

"There's gon' be some stuff you see that's gonna make it hard to smile in the future. But through whatever you see, through all the rain and the pain, you gotta keep your sense of humor, you gotta be able to smile through all the bullshit" —Tupac

THE LAST DRIVE

NATHAN WRIGHT

As I sit in the car waiting to leave my friend Daniel's house, I quickly scroll through my Facebook news feed. I see a status that catches my eye and do a double take.

My heart drops. Everything stops.

Jerett is in the hospital, they can't find Mikey.

Questions run through my head as I anxiously try to figure out what happened.

Where is Mikey? Why can't they find my cousin?

I quickly jump out of the car to call my mom and tell her the news. As I get out, Daniel shoots me a surprised look, wondering what the hell is going on.

"Have you heard anything about Mikey?" I ask her, fighting to keep my voice calm.

Silence. *She has no clue what I'm talking about.*

"I'll call you back in a minute," she says, rushing to get off the phone.

I wipe the sweat off my forehead as I clumsily light my cigarette. My hands are all clammy and I grip my phone tightly, waiting for my mom to call me back with some good news.

My phone rings, it's my cousin Michaela. I'm thinking the worst. I'm not ready for what she is going to say.

"What happened?" I demand. "Is Mikey still here?"

"He was in a serious car crash. He was drunk. He's not here with us no more," she says softly. I can tell she feels sorry for me.

"You fucking retard, you fucking retard, you fucking retard," I repeat over and over again out loud, wishing Mikey could hear me. Wishing it wasn't true.

⚜

When Mikey arrived in his Miata he was blaring Immortal Technique as loud as he could. As I got in I smelled power bait and looked down to see streaks of the rainbow colors running down his legs. His hair was greasy and he looked like he had just woken up from a long night of drinking.

We both looked at the sweltering temperature gauge: ninety-nine degrees. We decided to take the top of the car off as the sweat rolled down our faces. We were on our way to go fishing, but we decided it was too hot and we needed to go swimming instead.

We drove for a while with the sun beating down on the car, wanting so badly to get in the water. When we finally got to where the dirt road was blocked off, we had to get out and walk. As we walked down the road in the burning heat, Mikey took his shirt off—revealing all of the scars on his back created by his step mom's endless pimple popping sessions.

After what seemed like hours, we finally got to the cliff above the lake. We looked over the drop-off excitedly and Mikey suddenly took everything out of his pockets.

"See you down there!" he yelled as he ran toward the cliff edge. The next thing I knew he was doing a front flip as he jumped.

"Jump!" he yelled at me when he finally resurfaced in the cool water.

"I don't remember the water being that far down!" I said, my heart pounding.

"Just do it, you pansy!" he answered in his usual smart-ass tone.

I counted to three in my head, took a couple of steps back and started running, propelling myself off the cliff face. As I fell I felt free, with nothing in the world to worry about except spending time with my favorite cousin.

✳

My eyes are blurry with tears as I hang up the phone and get back in the car, slowly trying to come to terms with reality.

My heart starts pounding with rage. All I can think of is little Kash.

Why didn't he stop driving drunk when he had a child?

By the time we pull away from Daniel's house, my cigarette is gone. Daniel turns towards me in the back seat and hands me another.

"I think you need this," he says, trying to make me feel better.

As we drive in silence to Daniel's mom's house, I think back on the first time that Mikey rolled his car while driving drunk.

Why did he never learn?

Reality sinks in as we continue to drive and my anger turns back to sadness. I think back to all the times he ran off the road drunk, and all the drunken arguments he has had with the family. All the things that shouldn't have been said and now will never be said again.

I think about what my parents will say now that Mikey is gone. My family always told me not to look up to him, but I never wanted to listen. He always went out of his way to hang out with me and made me feel appreciated.

I remember when my dad sat me down one day for a talk. "He's not the person you want to look up to," he said. "He's not going to go far in life." These lectures never changed what I thought; nothing did.

Despite their warnings, every time I went to hang out with Mikey I'd tell my parents what I was doing. They wouldn't say anything besides "Be safe."

I know they thought he was a bad influence. I know they were worried about us being safe.

✦

It was midnight as I stood on the road in front of Grandma's with my cousin, Josh, waiting for Mikey to pick us up. He was always late.

He finally pulled up, looking a mess. I could tell that he didn't want to tell us what we were going to do that night. As Josh and I walked towards the car, he pulled off ahead like he was leaving without us. He was being a smart ass, laughing way too hard for the joke.

I got in the front seat, excited to leave on another adventure. As we drove, I looked back and saw two five-gallon buckets and huge flashlights in the back seat.

"We're going to get crawdads, "Mikey told us.

"OK," I answered, always ready to go with the flow with him.

We took a few turns and as soon as we hit a dirt road, I knew where we were. He pulled to the side of the road and got out, grabbing the buckets and flashlights.

"Watch out for their claws," Mikey said with a serious look as we walked down the incline to the canal.

I noticed that the water wasn't high enough to go through the culvert pipes under the road and crawdads were crawling all over the place. I could barely see the concrete under them, there were so many.

"They're everywhere!" I yelled.

"Told you so!" he laughed.

This was our favorite fishing spot because we could always catch something out of the spillway. That night the crawdads were big enough that we could just scoop them all up into the bucket.

The moon was so bright and high in the sky that our flashlights were pointless. The water was high enough that it washed over my toes. I wasn't surprised it was still warm from the burning sun of the day.

"Ahhhh!" Mikey yelled and I laughed at him, assuming he got bit. He yanked up his hand from the bucket with a crawdad clamped down on it.

As he flicked it off, I stood there laughing, feeling content. Any time spent with Mikey was the best of times for me.

✦

The rage and sadness of the situation continue to take over as we pull into Daniel's mom's driveway. I look out the window, feeling helpless, and see my sister waiting for me in her car.

I look down at my phone and see a text from her.

"We're going home."

I feel like I have no energy as I say goodbye to Daniel and drag my feet towards my sister's car. I get in and we just look at each other. Silence fills the air.

"I'm so sorry, Nate," she says sadly after a while, knowing how much this loss will affect me.

My mind is blank as we start the hour-long drive home. I stare out the window at the mountains and suddenly see a white sign on the side of the road. I know why it's there. My stomach turns as I read "Don't Drink and Drive" written in bold black letters on the white background. I scan the sign and underneath I see the list of names that no one ever wants to see a loved one on.

I'm motionless.

I can't believe my favorite person in the world has made that list.

✦

A Note from Nathan

The pain from the absence of losing my cousin doesn't decrease as time passes, but it comforts me to know he is watching over me. My family is going to the tree where the accident happened on the anniversary of his death this year to celebrate the memories he left behind. He will forever be in our hearts. Even from beyond the grave, my cousin left me one of the most important life lessons: to never drink and drive. I am now 17, a junior in high school. I plan to go to college and get a degree in environmental studies. I think about my cousin often, and I plan on getting a tattoo to remember him by. I will tell my future children his story and about the impact he had on my life.

"Someone has to die in order that the rest of us should value life more."—Virginia Woolf

THE CYCLE

JULIAN MARKFIELD

I walk into the living room dressed only in sweatpants. The look on my mom's face reflects disappointment and worry. She's assuming I only came out of my room for food, but I don't care much about that. The truth is I'm scared to leave my house. I haven't been to any class but one in more than two weeks.

"I'll try to go today," I mumble. Her expression changes to one of hope. It's nice to see for a change.

"Well, get dressed then," she says quickly. "I'm ready to leave when you are."

As I finish getting ready, I stand by the door and watch her put on the black Velcro- strapped wrist braces she wears for support every time she leaves the house. Her clothes are loose and baggy; she's wearing the same blue jeans and grey fuzzy zip-up sweatshirt as always. Life hasn't been easy for her, either.

I walk to the car ahead of her and set my backpack between my feet. I feel guilty making her drive me to and from school instead of doing the things she needs to do. She turns on the car and starts to pull out of the parking space.

"We can stop at Jimmy John's for lunch since you missed it at school," she says in her soothing, motherly voice.

I quietly mumble "Sure." "Thank you" follows a few minutes later.

As we approach the school, the feelings of anxiety return. My stomach drops. My hands shake. My heart feels like I just drank a gallon of coffee. *What am I thinking? How can I do this? Why don't I just stay at home and sleep?*

"Mom…" I whisper.

"What?" she sighs.

"I can't do it."

It's silent inside the car. Outside, I hear kids walking by, talking and laughing with each other. I don't even want to look at my mom.

"You're going," she says." You've already missed seventy-two days of school. You're not missing another."

I take a deep breath. I can't make myself get out of the car. I start planning how I'm going to convince her to let me go back home.

"What's so hard about going to school?"

I get asked this question a lot. Once I started missing it became an endless cycle of convincing myself the night before I had to go, then waking up and staying in bed no matter how much I knew I shouldn't. I woke up feeling depressed and unmotivated. It was impossible to get out of bed, and the worst part was I was clueless about why.

Some people thought I must be having fun staying home. They were wrong. They didn't understand that I was stuck in bed and hating myself for being there. I fought with my parents all day and all night. I had to go to court. I was miserable.

On the days I did go to school, my first period teacher singled me out for not having been in class. One day, she made me sit on the floor in the corner and announced to everyone it was because I skipped school. I tried to explain to her that I had back issues and it pained me to sit there, but all she said was, "Don't miss school and you won't have to."

Nobody knew I was struggling with depression. It was a secret I hid. Kids started to criticize me:

"Why do you miss so much school?"

"Everyone else can go to school; all you have to do is get up. It's not that hard."

"Wow! You're actually at school today!"

While to them these were harmless jokes, to me they felt like punches in the chest. I had gotten up and beaten the depression that morning, only to be made fun of.

I couldn't explain that depression wasn't something I could just push away. I didn't want people to know how depression had poisoned my mind and made it seem physically impossible to defy, or that it clouded my thinking until I believed I couldn't do anything. How could I admit that I was resigned to being a failure?

Eventually, school was so stressful that I would fake throwing up so I could go home. My mom would grudgingly come get me and we'd either have a silent car ride or argue the whole way home. I felt sick that even my own parents—who had always sided with me and understood—were turning against me. The people who themselves had chronic depression and had passed on the same genes to me couldn't understand what I was going through. It took so much not to scream at them. I thought about it, though. I planned out the whole scene:

"This is complete bullshit! Why the fuck can't you understand how hard this is?" I wanted to shout. In my mind I would go to my room, pack my bag full of clothes, food, and anything else I might need, and storm out of the house. I would sleep at my old abandoned house for who knows how long, even though I had been completely terrified of it since I was little.

But when the moment came, I could never get the words out. I would just stomp off to my room and try not to break anything.

One time I remember the arguments getting so bad that I punched a hole straight through my laundry room door and then—so I didn't get in more trouble—I punched the ground until I couldn't handle the pain.

I began to enjoy the sight of my blood. It was interesting to watch it trickle down my skin. Sometimes while I showered I took a scrub brush and rubbed it against my knuckles until the water dripping off them was tinged pink. I tried to explain this to the people I thought were my friends, but then they spread rumors that I was emo and liked to fill up the bathtub with my blood. This, of course, made me want to stay home even more.

"Julian, are you going to get out of the car? I have to go to work."

"Yeah, sure," I mumble. I get out of the car and glance around. Four hours of school left in the day. Four hours of dealing with bullies, teachers yelling at me, feeling excluded, depressed and scared. My heart races as I begin to open the big, red double doors. I look back at my mom in the car. The smile is gone from her face. She realizes that I'm not going to be able to go inside. Deep down I think she knew this from the start, but she wanted to believe in me. She hoped I would break the cycle.

I hear the heavy doors close behind me as I walk slowly back to the car. I slump into the seat and my mind begins to shut down. As my mom begins the long drive home, I prepare for yet another argument.

I will try again tomorrow.

Note from Julian

I continued to struggle for the final month of middle school, though I tried very hard to attend my Woods and Metals class. My teacher, Mr. Seymour, inspired me to show up because he believed I could succeed. It was the only class I passed that semester. I'm now in ninth grade and besides excused absences due to health issues, I've done so well the judge recently excused my truancy case. Making the choice to attend Scriber has been the best choice for me; the small class sizes and encouraging teachers have helped me learn to overcome my problems and attend school regularly.

"However difficult life may seem, there is always something you can do and succeed at."—Stephen Hawking

FACING MY DEMONS

LILLY ANDERSON

I stand staring at a sunken-in face with no light in her eyes; she looks like she is slowly going to waste. The puffy dark circles insist she hasn't slept in days, and with her tiny bones and baggy clothes, she also looks like she hasn't eaten. At 5'4 and only 90 pounds, I'm sure people are starting to get concerned about her. The more I focus, the more I can see that this stranger in the mirror is actually me.

I grasp the edge of the counter as my lips start to quiver. My eyes begin to overflow because I never thought I'd end up here. Only one day sober; it's almost hard to believe. This time I'm pretty sure I was high for more a week. I'm finally ready to get clean, but my demons are still calling. *Life is too much, we know you can feel the pressure. Cave in now, come on you know it only takes one hit to feel better.*

I need to find a way to escape my head; these voices are really starting to interfere with my thought process. They are waiting, surrounding and suffocating, pushing me to break. But instead I lock the door behind me and turn the faucet on cold. I suck up my tears and splash my face, doing everything possible to distract myself from the cravings in my brain. I grab the zebra towel and pat my face dry. *Why did I let myself fall in so deep? How did I let this evil take so much control over me?* I rest my back against the wall, slowly slide down and curl up on the floor. My eyes fill with tears again and this time I decide to let them fall. I lay my head in my knees because my fuzzy pajama pants will soak them all up.

I remember it like it was yesterday, like there have been no days in between. The day that changed me forever, tainting me at barely sixteen. The day I met the monster.

It was half-way through day number two on the extremely crowded boat. I was dripping sweat and I could still feel the hangover from the day before lingering in my throat. It was Seafair, a summer festival in Seattle, and my mom had snuck me on board. Everyone thought I was of age, so nobody felt the need to try to watch over me. I grabbed what was left in the fruity-smelling cup and downed the last of the vodka.

My mind was still completely present, so I went in search of something better than the beer I could find. Thinking back to the day before, I remembered a guy in the back room who had given me some coke. I found my way back, pushing through the crowds of people, dodging the creeps who probably didn't mind copping a feel. I was surrounded by some crazy people. Everyone reeked of body odor and the girls thought it was okay to drop their tops and reveal. All they got for this were just some cheap beads, but it almost seemed like they were claiming a medal, one they were proud to receive.

I finally found my way to the back of the yacht and waved to my mom who was on the bow mingling with the two people who had brought us aboard. She replied with a loud "Hello," her long pointed nails reflecting sparkles as she waved.

Right then I realized I hadn't seen her since we pushed off land. I climbed down the blue-carpeted stairs. The lower level was huge. It held a kitchen and bathroom—someone could live down there. I took in a deep breath before taking the last couple of steps, unsure of what was about it happen. I barely knew the guy or what he was capable of so I hesitated a little before knocking on the bedroom door.

He opened it just a crack.

"Is there anything left"? I asked, feeling the butterflies in my stomach. My cheeks slowly began to burn.

"I have something, but it's not the same," he replied. His straggly black hair fell in front of his face, but his sunken-in cheekbones were his most dominant feature. "If you really want some I will share anyway." His answer intrigued me so I nodded my head.

Before I knew it I was in the room. He shut and locked the door behind me and my heart began to race. My thoughts were going everywhere—I was praying I hadn't made a mistake. But to my surprise and relief there were already two girls taking advantage of his drugs. That definitely made me feel a little bit better; at least I knew I wasn't about to get raped. I looked at them as they blew out smoke, the clouds huge and mesmerizing.

"You can smoke this clear. It's your choice," he said. "But no matter how fun it seems, remember it's easy to lose sight."

"I can handle it," I said, my voice shaking. The only thing on my mind at that moment was getting high.

"This drug is very addicting," he continued. "Trust me, hun, it ruined me."

"Give me the pipe," I said. His serious gaze turned into a dangerous grin. Without hesitation he handed it to me.

"Let me teach you. Spin it slow, let it melt." The little clear bubble slowly started to fill with smoke.

"Suck slowly," he said as I put it to my lips. I inhaled for as long as I could. As soon as I exhaled, jitters raced through my body in one big jolt. It was the best feeling ever, like something out of a movie. Everything felt perfect—the way I thought I should feel every day. I actually felt happy. Even with all the warnings, it was amazing. In that moment, I didn't believe it was evil. To me, it felt more like the work of one of heaven's angels.

One hit and it implanted itself into my brain. I never wanted to come down. It was my new escape, and started to cover up all the pain I didn't want to face. I had been a ticking time bomb waiting to self-destruct, doing everything in my power to make the voices stop. The voices were constantly yelling into my ear, making me want do things no person should ever endure—like running a blade across my skin and skipping meals days on end.

The self-hatred had gotten so strong that I spent the majority of my life trying to shake it off. This drug was like a discovery; I felt that maybe it could solve it all. It could keep my life moving forward and keep me standing up when I felt I was about to fall.

The strangers in that room now felt like close friends. The four of us wasted the night, lost in our own little world, talking about life. As we passed around the pipe, our minds were stuck on hyper-speed. We didn't even notice that the boat was heading back and that it was almost time to leave. When I exited the room I finally felt alive, almost high enough to touch the sky.

I walked across the hall to the bathroom and when I looked in the mirror, I saw that the light in my eyes had gone dim. My hands were sweaty and a huge mischievous grin covered my face.

I made my way back up the blue steps, seeing each fiber of the carpet—every strand. Things were so vivid, different as a whole. The world was so much more beautiful now, and I had no idea it was possible. Life felt unreal.

As the waves threw us around, I stumbled across the boat. I wasn't ready to let this feeling go, so once again I found the man from the back room—the guy who had just taken what was left of my youth.

"I don't want to go home yet. I still want to have fun," I explained.

He handed me the pipe. "Give me your phone," he said.

I did as instructed and watched as he put his number in my contacts.

"Leave your phone on loud and I will come by and grab the pipe at the end of the night."

With that I was on my way home and heading toward addiction.

I've been staring at the stranger's reflection for almost an hour now. I'm sick of this lifestyle and I want to do better. I'm finished. I refuse to let this monster do more damage than it's already done. I turn the sink on warm and grab a cloth from under the counter. I clean off the remaining makeup smears and all the dried-up tears. I am determined to do more with my life, to re-learn to live without the high. *I am better than this; I know what I'm worth.* I slowly start to see the light replenish itself back into my eyes before I turn the bathroom light off and take a deep breath. I am finally ready to stop giving into the demons inside my head. I am ready to face my fears and put up a fight. I am determined now. This war will be mine.

A Note from Lilly

I have been sober ever since that day, and it's been a lot easier to enjoy life than I thought it would be. I have learned that everything is about perspective; even tragedy comes with something positive in it. Sometimes it is hard to find, but I have discovered it's a lot better to live looking on the bright side. Right now I am a graduating senior and plan to go to cosmetology school. Doing hair has been my dream for as long as I can remember and I am hoping to open a salon one day.

"It's a metaphor, you see: you put the killing thing right between your teeth but you don't give it the power to do its killing."—John Green, The Fault in Our Stars *(Augustus Waters)*

LOSING IT

DELANIE HIGBEE

I stare deeply at my hands. I examine every tiny cut, scratch and wrinkle that covers the skin on my palms and fingers, up to my wrists where the wounds are puffy, red and hand-made.

Click.Click. I press a thumb down on the top of the pen I'm holding, running my gaze along the clip. I study the small white letters that spell out "Bic."

Trigger, I think to myself. I'd kill for a cigarette. I wish more than anything that I could light a Marb and fill my lungs with smoke, then squeeze it out and watch the white clouds drip off my lips and vanish.

I'd kill for any sense of normality. It's only day two. *How the hell am I going to survive another five days?*

My inner voices are screaming, I can feel my eardrums pulse. *I want out, I want out, I need out.* Anxiety rattles my body. I pull my lips behind my teeth and bite down, holding my mouth shut so I don't leak out a scream.

"What are the three R's?" the counselor asks with a smile, as if she's happy to be here. I roll my eyes. *NO. Not again. Please.* It's the same speech from yesterday, and the same speech I'll hear three times a day for the next five days. Hands shoot up across the room.

"Respect yourself! Respect your community! Respect others!" a young girl exclaims.

I begin another full-circle eye roll.

The room is L-shaped and very slim. It's crowded with kids draped over dark blue plastic furniture lining bright yellow walls. There's nothing *other* than plastic furniture and kids around here. There are locks on every door and constant banging and yelling coming from other wings. I'm sitting at the table in the corner of the L, trying to tune out the noise.

My stomach rumbles and my numbness is broken. I lift my head to see Jay staring towards me, but it's not me he's looking at. It's the door seven feet behind me. As long as he's focused there, he won't notice me looking at him.

Jay was brought in almost twenty-four hours after me, and so far every feeling I've had about being forced to stay here I witnessed him experience a day later. I felt closest to him because he was friendly and I could relate to him. He looked so much like Chase from *Zoey 101*; his eyes were icy blue and his short curly wannabe Afro laid flat on his head, like stepped-on grass.

Jake told me the story behind the meltdown that led him to join me in this plastic hell: he'd tried to end his life over a girl he'd loved for two years and didn't think he could live without. He was shocked to learn she wanted to live without *him*.

I felt sick knowing he had gone through the same feelings of hopelessness I had when I wanted to end *my* life—for the same reason. Nothing hurts as much as your first love telling you she doesn't love you anymore, and it felt like a weight being pulled off my shoulders when I heard Jay describe it. I realized I wasn't insane for holding on so tightly to a girl who didn't love me anymore. After hearing his story, I felt okay for a moment, and I hadn't felt okay for a very long time.

Looking at him now reminds me that I'm the normal amount of "dysfunctional," and it helps me deal with what I tried to do to myself. His lips press together for a short moment before I see his teeth peek out. I see the small gap between his front teeth, then the rest of his crooked smile. He sees my vacant stare and gives me a smirk.

I hear the unlocking beep the door makes when a staff member enters, but I'm not interested in turning around. Although Jay's story brought me some peace, it didn't make my girlfriend love me. I still feel empty—of food, of thought, and of hope. I don't want to be here. I don't want to be alive. I just want to disappear.

"Jay, you have a visitor," a voice announces behind me. His mother squeezes in between me and another kid at the table and hands him a McDonald's bag.

"Thank god." He exhales his words loudly, pulls a Big Mac from the bag and opens the box it rests in. I watch him admire it while the kids around him drool. He lifts it to his eyes, but before his lips can touch it, an angry voice growls behind me:

"Give. Me. That. Burger."

The words don't alert Jay because he's intent on taking a monstrous bite. The source of the voice, a boy named Dillon, leaps from the ground, stepping on my thigh to lift himself onto the table. He slides towards Jay and grabs at the Big Mac box. My jaw falls open as Dillon claws at the food. It's entertaining. But I'm also worried for Jay's safety. Dillon has full-blown crazy eyes.

Counselors begin to evacuate kids onto the outside patio for their safety, but I don't plan to get up anytime soon. I watch Jay swipe his burger off the table and jump up like a prairie dog popping out of its hole; he looks alert like a prairie dog, too. He leans backwards towards the wall to escape Dillon's reach, but Dillon crawls onto a chair and stands up, making them eye level. I've never seen this kid still for more than a second. I'm witnessing an intense amount of concentration for someone who's always been energetic and destructive. The stare-down lasts for maybe twenty seconds, but it feels like five minutes. Even I feel the threat.

"GIVE IT TO ME!" Dillon screams desperately. He is inches away from Jay's face now, but it's clear this child is no match.

I watch Jay's face go from shock to fear to being completely over it. He starts to walk away. Fixing his eyes on Jay, Dillon pushes himself off of the chair, wraps his arms around his neck and climbs onto his back. Jay continues to act like he couldn't care less. Burger in hand, he continues walking with Dillon dangling from his back.

I stand up to follow the action and the group. I walk up close to Jay, not letting him out of my sight. As Dillon clings to him, screaming, Jay looks annoyed but not angry.

Witnessing Dillon out of control reminds how out of control *I* had been and how much my emotions got the best of me. Dillon was letting his desires dictate his actions. It was all too familiar to me.

I'm not walking anymore, and realize I'm all by myself in the L-shaped room. Suddenly I have an epiphany: *I know what I did was a mistake, a moment of weakness. But I want to be here. I want to be on this earth.* I feel myself coming back from the grey void of hopelessness.

This won't be the end of my depression. I know I have a difficult journey ahead, but I have control of my life from here. I will not be the victim of my emotions. I will find the strength to push through my sadness. I *will* rise up.

❧

A Note from Delanie

I was admitted to the Inpatient Psychiatric Unit at Children's Hospital a year ago. Honestly, I'm not sure how to explain why I thought suicide was my only option, but I can say it wasn't all because of this situation. I've struggled with depression my entire life and some days it gets the best of me. Depression is a mental illness and it's not something you will just one day overcome. When you're young you think this is everything, it's right now or never. Everything feels like the most important thing. That may be how you feel, but it's not the truth. You're young and experiencing these things for the first time. You're expected to just learn from it, deal with it and move on. At the time of this story, I wasn't in a healthy mindset and couldn't deal with my emotions. I made a mistake, but I don't regret it. Being in the IPU was an amazing experience. At first I hated it more than anything, but it taught me how to cope. Much like writing this story, it gave me some power over my emotions that I didn't have before. I used to feel like a victim to my negative thoughts and feelings, but now I've learned to distract myself and step back from the situation. I've learned Right Now isn't everything. I have so many more days and years to live, so much more to experience, and an endless number of things to learn. I'm still in a relationship with my first love, and in September we will be celebrating two years together. Love isn't easy, but we wouldn't be in love if we didn't stay by each other's sides. There is always hope and things are always changing. I swear on my life, things do get better.

"It gets better."—Dan Savage

WHAT WAS I THINKING?

VLAD KOVALSKY

I'm sitting in a cold holding room, listening to footsteps behind a heavy metal door. It's past midnight, and one thought runs through my head: *Why did I do this?*

My body feels like an ice cube in the middle of a cold, cold ocean. The cops have taken my sweatshirt and shoes.

"This kid really screwed up his life," I hear someone in the next room say.

All I can think of is how stupid I am for trying to pull off this stunt.

William had just taken a few hits from the pipe Greg and I had smoked during our walk to the Alderwood Mall. It was early November and even in my North Face down coat, I was cold.

I turned my back away from the wind and shoved my hands into my pockets.

"You guys want to pull off a job?"

I glanced over at William. I was confused by his words—it must have been the high talking—and at first I thought he was joking.

"What job?" Greg and I asked. We headed back into the mall and as we walked slowly past Zumiez and Hot Topic, William detailed what he had in mind. He wanted us to go to Nordstrom and steal some high-priced watches. I felt my gut tighten. He wasn't acting like this was a joke.

I looked at Greg to see if he would say something, but he just looked back at me with a blank, scared expression. I turned to face William.

"There's no way I'm doing that," I told him.

"Pussy!" he hissed.

"Dickhead." My muscles tensed.

William increased his taunts. "You're a pussy. A pussy. Pussy. Pussy. Pussy."

I looked at Greg and saw he had the same fear in his eyes. But he was dead silent. I felt the pressure building inside my head. I hated it when people called me names. I walked ahead of William, trying to ignore him, but the taunts continued.

"Pussy. Pussy. That's what you are. A pussy."

Greg continued to stay silent. I knew he was scared, but why wasn't he standing up for me? The insults kept coming and I couldn't shut them out.

"You're a stupid fuck!" I hissed.

I saw his fist flying toward me, but was too late to stop it; he punched me dead center in the stomach. His punch pushed the air out of my lungs. I knew then that William wasn't a real friend, only someone who wanted Greg and me to pull off this stupid job for him.

"Pussies can't call *me* names," he said.

William was bigger than I was, at least six-foot two, and older. I was scared of him. I knew that if I tried to resist, he would just hurt me more.

"Fine, I'll do it," I said.

As William explained the plan, I felt my world caving in on me. The idea of stealing was nauseating and I felt a heavy weight slowly crushing my insides at the thought of what I was about to do. His annoying, high-pitched voice continued when all I really wanted to hear was silence.

We headed toward Nordstrom and scouted around. William scanned the cases. The Michael Kors and G-Shock watches caught his eye. Once he knew what to come back to, we left Nordstrom and walked toward the food court.

"Do you guys know what you're going for?" he asked, staring down at us.

I stood near Panda Express, my adrenaline piling up, waiting to explode. I looked at Greg. I could tell he was as scared as I was. I knew what he was thinking. He was thinking the same thing *I* was thinking. *Are we really going to do this? Is it really worth it?*

We headed back toward Nordstrom, walked into the store and approached the case of watches. *This is it.* We each grabbed a box and the adrenaline that had piled up quickly released itself through my body. My head felt hot. Everywhere I looked there were tracers behind displays. It was hard to focus on anything. We walked past the security detectors and immediately heard a loud DING DING DING.

The three of us started sprinting through the mall's parking lot. My vision blurred and everything around me faded away.

"Don't stop running!" William screamed.

All I wanted to *do* was stop running and punch him in the face. I ran toward the only thing I could see, a trail directly in front of me. I couldn't see anything except this one way out. I looked back and saw three fat security guards chasing us. Everything was going just as I expected: horribly.

We ran on and the only thing I felt was pain from head to toe. My entire body ached but I couldn't stop running. If I stopped now, it was over.

We ran across a busy four-way street. Luckily none of us got hit. I wish William *had* been, to be honest. At that moment, I hated him that much. We ran for about a half-mile at least. Non-stop sprinting.

We finally decided to rest in a forest next to the old Lynnwood High.

We sat there for what felt like thirty minutes but it was really only about four. Three words bounced around my head:

FUCK YOU WILLIAM.

I felt a warm sensation in my throat and started humming to make it go away. The humming made it worse. I threw up on William's shoes.

"What the fuck, dude?" he yelled as he dragged a shoe's toe in the grass.

I kept my mouth shut but really the only thing I want to do was punch him in the jaw as hard as I could. My vomit covered his black Air Jordans with red lining. I laughed a little inside.

We stood up. We walked through the forest and ended up in a neighborhood.

"Hey, get on the ground now!" A cop stood behind me. My hands shook and my torso froze.

William and I climbed over a seven-foot wooden fence in front of us and Greg started running in a different direction. We ran through a backyard.

"We got one of them!" we heard in the distance.

That's when I knew Greg was done.

William and I ran into the street. He saw a cop car and whispered, "Hide, Bro!" We hid underneath a bush, staying dead silent. I lay there completely still, but my heart was racing. We heard footsteps about fifteen feet away and saw black leather boots walking slowly toward us. The only thing going through my head was *Fuck You William.*

It was over. All over.

The cop pointed his gun and flashlight at both of us.

"Come out with your hands up!" he screamed.

We crawled out of the bush with our hands in the air. I saw three cops pointing their guns at me. One approached me from the side and clamped cuffs on my wrists. He started pushing me around and asking questions like "Why did you do this?" and "Who made you do this?"

I told the police that William made Greg and me pull this off. That didn't change anything, though. The cop led me to his car, dumped me in the back seat and drove away.

Now I'm sitting here in this tiny, freezing-cold room hearing faint footsteps. My adrenaline is slowly going away, but I feel so depressed because I know nothing good will come from this. Four thoughts keep running through my head: The first three are "I Hate You So Much William," "Why did I listen to you?" and "What are my parents going to do?" But the one that comes back most often is "What was I thinking?"

Note from Vlad

I regret this stunt from last November. I had to go to court and was relieved not to have to go to jail. I'm back at school and my grades are better than before. This experience changed my view on peer pressure—some people say it only affects little kids but really it affects everyone. No matter what kind of peer pressure, stick to your word. Say No. My plan is to go to Shoreline Community College to become a mechanic.

"What screws us up the most in life is the picture in our head of how it is supposed to be."—Anonymous

CAPITAL STEEZ

ZEKE SMITH

I glance out the window of the Beemer and can tell the sunlight will be completely gone within an hour.

This only adds to my anxiety as we drive through a suburban neighborhood with three-story houses and perfectly landscaped yards.

The turn signal makes a final click and we pull into a long driveway next to a huge, colonial-style house. The music on the stereo slows to a soft murmur of trumpet sounds and comforting soulful singing, yet my legs are shaking and I can't make them stop.

I look from Jose—the older guy with the weathered face sitting next to me—to the .22 gun in my lap. The stainless steel reflects the fading light of the day and creates an amber tone along the slide.

My knuckles turn white as the steel begins to warm. I'm nervous about two people on the other side of that perfect-looking house—the ones who asked for seven rifles and a duffle bag full of ammunition. But that's not what has me shaking.

I'm shaking because I'm scared of disappointing Jose. I don't want him to know that I'm thinking this will be the last time I help him; I'm not sure how he'll respond. Over the past year, I've become his go-to guy. He's even hinted that he's grooming me to take over his business.

I sit up in my seat and concentrate on making my demeanor so firm he won't notice.

He looks at me intently. "You cool, Guey?"

I nod. But as we take the two duffle bags out of the trunk and head

- 118 -

toward the house, I feel a lot more than the weight of the guns and the ammo. I feel the weight of my girlfriend's words bearing down on me.

"You know you're better than getting into this. You're a better person than the violence that these guns give. Their sole purpose is to kill efficiently. You're helping this cause."

I can hear the loose rounds of ammo jiggle in their boxes and feel the pull of the barrel of a rifle.

I run my hand over the .22 tucked against my body and look over at Jose to make sure his Glock is in easy reach. Then I knock on the door, ready for whatever's about to go down.

I first knew Jose as one of my mom's friends. He'd come over to drink beer and hang out with her and her boyfriend. He was an older guy, fifty-ish, who worked as a bartender as far as I knew. His skin was sun-bleached and he looked as if he had been working in the fields his whole life—or doing a lot of drugs. I got a shifty vibe from him at first, but didn't think my mom would put herself around bad people. I figured he was cool and trustworthy.

One night I was watching "Frasier," trying to bore myself into sleep. The TV volume was off and the bluish tint of the light made a stark contrast with the burning embers at the end of the joint I was smoking. I exhaled deeply and rested my head on the living-room couch. I heard the chatter between my mom and her friends in the next room. I heard footsteps and looked up to see Jose standing near the couch.

"Why you still up?" he asked in a heavy accent.

I shrugged. "I go to bed when I want to."

"You smokin'?"

I passed him my joint and noticed him staring at the silent TV.

"I watch without the sound so I can see what's really going on," I explained.

"I used to watch movies like that all the time," he said. "We had a dial TV and the sound didn't work but our house got good enough reception to get all the channels."

I was annoyed to be bothered so late, but then again, most of my mom's friends didn't talk to me at all. "Where are you from?" I asked, curious about his accent.

Jose sat down on the arm of the couch. "Nicaragua. I moved up here as soon as I had the money."

Now I was intrigued. "Why?" I asked.

"Nicaragua isn't a bad place. There are just too many bad people. I was tired of feeling like I was putting my own people down."

"What do you mean by 'putting your people down'?"

He took a few hits off the joint and passed it back to me.

"In Nicaragua, it's tough for the average man to make money. The cartels have all the money and they don't treat us so good."

"You worked for a cartel?" I asked. Now he *really* had my interest.

Jose pulled out his phone and scrolled down through some contacts. "See this one right here?"

I leaned over to look at the contact number and read: *Pozolero*. He explained that this guy was the coroner for the cartels. Basically, his job was getting rid of bodies without a funeral. I shot him a what-the-fuck look.

"If I call this person," he continued, "I can get anything I want. Molta, cuetes, yeyo. Anything, Guey."

An idea was forming in my head. If Jose could afford drugs and anything else he wanted, then he was doing more than bartending.

"You've got guns?" I asked hopefully.

He motioned for me to follow him out the front door. His 2001 BMW 328i was parked in the driveway. My eyes sparkled when he opened the trunk. I stared down at a black nine-millimeter Glock. I was mesmerized. All I could think about was feeling the ribs in the silver slide. As if reading my mind, Jose picked up the pistol and put it in my hands. I smiled, thinking of the security it could bring to my mom and older brother.

I was only fourteen but I knew all about our family's financial problems. My brother and my mom both worked hard. And then there were the bruises I had seen more than a few times on my mom's arms. I was tired of feeling like a kid who couldn't do anything to contribute to the family. I couldn't bring in any money, and I certainly couldn't protect my mom from the men she went out with. This was more than a gun I was holding. It was a whole lot of solutions.

For the first time in my life, I felt like I had some power. "How does someone even get something like this?"

Jose looked at me and nodded slowly. I could tell he was thinking he could help me take care of my family the way that someone back in Nicaragua might have helped him.

"You want to get one of your own, Guey?"

I looked up and nodded. Jose took back the heavy Glock, then reached into his trunk and pulled out a weathered Walther PPK nine-millimeter short pistol.

It felt just right in my hands.

Five days after our last job—one that netted me nearly $1,000, cash—I still haven't worked up the nerve to tell Jose I'm through. But now it's Thursday night and I know he's got another gun run set up for the

WE HOPE YOU RISE UP

weekend.

I have to tell him. I promised Ridley I was done with this life.

I enter the dive bar and head to the back where Jose works as a bartender. I hear his reggae blaring and find him standing just outside the back door, smoking a cigarette.

"What's going on?" he says when he sees me.

"Nothing man, I just came to kick it with you," I lie.

"I'm off in fifteen." Juan tosses his Beemer keys to me. "Warm her up for me and we can go chill at your place."

It's a long drive back to my house. We talk about nothing for most of the way, but as the exit signs on the freeway whiz past, I feel my gut tighten. I've got to get this over with.

"Jose, there's something I want to talk to you about," I say finally, forcing the words out of my mouth.

"Quianda, Guey?"

"I'm getting out."

He is silent for what seems like hours and it makes me think about taking back what I've just said.

"Okay, Guey," he says softly. He sounds not exactly pissed-off like I expected, but sad.

Relief washes over me.

"Sorry, Bro, it's my girlfriend, Ridley. She heard about Marco getting shot," I say, starting to apologize. Marco had been working for Jose, helping him deliver guns—the same as me. He was only twenty-four when he died. "I'm sorry…"

"It's cool, Guey," Juan interrupts. "It's just that I thought I could depend on you to step up and take on responsibility. You were going to be my way out."

"I appreciate all you've done for me and my family over the past year," I say. And it's true. The money has helped a lot and I feel guilty for deserting him. In some ways, he feels like my family.

But now, Ridley's family to me, too. She's the first person in my life that has really been there to support me one hundred percent. I've never had someone who expected me to be responsible and do the right thing.

I have to get out. Not just for me, but for her.

❖

A Note from Zeke

I've been out for a year and a half now. Working full time for my income has been difficult, but I enjoy my job at Moonshine BBQ, and my relationship with Ridley has never been stronger. I feel great knowing that I'm making money the right way and supporting myself. I'm starting college this spring and saving up to fulfill my dream of owning an AE86 with a fully tuned 4AGE and a N2 body kit. The title to my story is in tribute to Jamal Dewar Jr.

"He is richest who is content with the least, for content is the wealth of nature."—Socrates

WHO WE ARE

Very top by sign: Santino Dewyer. Back row: Dave Zwaschka, Jen Haupt, Kai Lee, Zeke Smith, Ridley Peterson, Marjie Bowker, Brieaunna Dacruz, Kenny Kelly, Delanie Higbee, Jeff Kauk, Vlad Kovalsky, Nathan Wright, Cyrena Fulton. Middle row: Danielle Anthony-Goodwin, Ingrid Ricks, Destiny Allison, Julian Markfield. Bottom row: Jaycee Schrenk, Isabel Cordova, Kathy Clift, Lilly Anderson, Haylee Pearson, Emma Hess, Breanna Pratt.

Scriber Lake High School is in the Edmonds School District, located just north of Seattle, Washington. Our school is not alternative but it is one of choice; some students start their freshman year, others come later seeking a second chance, and some land here for a last chance. We are a school of small classrooms and attentive teachers who not only care about our education but also our personal lives. At Scriber we focus on experiences that motivate us to set heart-and-soul goals for the future.

The Scriber staff has written a book called *Creating a Success Culture: Transforming our Schools One Question at a Time.* It is about our quest to empower students by using 17 questions designed to bring them back into the center of their own education. It is available on Amazon.

ABOUT THIS PROGRAM

This book project was facilitated through Write to Right, a program that fosters healing, literacy and understanding through personal storytelling. The student writing and publishing program was co-founded by Scriber Lake English teacher Marjie Bowker and Seattle memoir author Ingrid Ricks, who have been using narrative writing to help students find their voice and power since January 2012.

Write to Right is committed to helping educators implement this Common Core program through its comprehensive narrative writing and publishing curriculum, as well as through teacher training workshops and writer-in-residence programs designed to help pilot the program and provide one-on-one student mentoring. We also offer presentations on the power of personal storytelling.

For more information, please visit www.writetoright.org

ACKNOWLEDGMENTS

This student writing/publishing program would not be possible without the backing of the Edmonds School District and the ongoing encouragement and support of Scriber Lake principal, Kathy Clift. From the beginning, she has understood the power of these voices and the importance of ensuring that they are heard.

We are grateful to the Hazel Miller Foundation and the Apex/Bruce and Jolene McCaw Family Foundation for awarding us grants that have funded this program. We are also grateful to Edmonds Community College, the Edmonds Kiwanis and the Rotary Club of Edmonds Daybreakers for their ongoing support of our students.

We want to extend a special thank you to Dave Zwaschka, Danielle Anthony-Goodwin and Jennifer Haupt, all gifted writers who donated their time, talent and hearts to help students in this year's publishing workshop revise and polish their stories. We also want to thank Carol Bowker, who volunteered her time to proofread this book. Finally, we'd like to thank Cafe Louvre for providing us a wonderful venue to host our book launch events.

Thank you all for helping to make this book possible.

CPSIA information can be obtained
at www.ICGtesting.com
Printed in the USA
FSOW01n0114180515
7101FS

9 780989 438124